MAE DESSAUVAGE

THE DOLLHOUSE

Blurring Books

The content of this publication could easily be approached from the perspective of an art historical journey. I could make a meandering, iconographic exploration back and forth between the past and the present and everything that lies somewhere in between. Other people are more skilled than I am at pursuing this kind of trans-historical approach with accuracy and precision. I prefer instead to focus on how I experienced the work of Mae Dessauvage from the first moment I came to discover it. That first encounter, at Tatjana Pieters in 2024, was one of wonder and fascination. I was drawn to the sophistication and elegance of the execution — both in the works on paper and on wooden panels. I should also mention the shrines, which echo the artist's interest in art history and architecture. A shrine, in the end, is nothing more than a way of keeping something dead alive. Anyway, in Mae's work, a quiet color scheme seems to be used to give birth to a figure that resonates as an archetype in each work. Every work is a silent, gentle scene evoking a small event — holding or gazing at a skull, holding a schematized profile of a church, a ball, a head… But, behind the gentleness, I sensed deeper layers of emotion, as if the figure had been created to cope with transformative events. Was I looking at an alter ego of the artist? An idealized self-portrait? Was this figure the narrator of a hidden story, to be completed by the spectator? My confrontation with the work of Mae Dessauvage opened a myriad of thoughts and associations. But above all, I was moved, emotionally touched. I am happy to say it so directly. At that moment, I had never met the artist and knew nothing of her biography or trajectory. Only the painted membrane of the works spoke to me, resonating with a different kind of nature. And this explains my refusal to lose myself in the intellectual exercise of an art historical reading. How nice it is just to accept the things in front of you as they are — inexplicable — and to embrace them intuitively. Before I forget, I would like to mention the book *Triptych – Three Studies on Francis Bacon* by Jonathan Littell. In his personal exploration of the work of Francis Bacon through three essays, Littell reflects at a certain point on old Russian Orthodox icons, noting that it seems as though you, as a spectator, are not looking at the paintings, but that the paintings are gazing at you. The direction of the gaze is inverted, giving the icon a kind of independent existence. A spectator is no longer needed; the figures in the painting look out on their own. Reading this passage brought me back to the work of Mae Dessauvage. Immediately after reading it, I looked at her work online, wondering what the eyes in her paintings do. In Mae's work, the eyes are larger than life, with their gaze not specifically fixed. They seem to remind us that we as spectators are part of something else. Mae's work is a dollhouse, as the title of this publication indicates. And within this dollhouse, the artist is both choreographer and creator of the doll's body — in pieces and as a whole — of the doll's interactions, of the gently layered narrative. Dolls have often been described as transitional objects, objects that give psychological comfort to children in new or unsettling situations. The reason that the doll gives comfort might be found in its imagined mute perfection. The doll's world is a mechanized, controlled world, in which the outside world is reflected but released from its narrow societal frameworks. In that sense, even the old icons could be understood as dolls. If we were to make an abstraction of their religious context, they could be seen as painted stand-ins for softening a complex world. Yet Mae's dollhouse is not an innocent paradise of stand-ins. It is haunted by the shadowy bodies surrounding the figures; it is a transformative body of work mediated through an artistic language in which everything seems to be a sketch (or prototype) of the dolls yet to be made. Finally, I want to return to a small but significant detail: in many works one will find short strokes of paint, one next to the other, a synthesis of the colors used in the work. They remind us that we are looking at a constructed world of moldable figures, one whose relevance is present for the artist and anyone who engages with the work. The work of Mae Dessauvage is, following my intuition, a mirror for herself. But it is also a mirror for me and every onlooker to reflect on the relationship with the self, the other, and the world we too often ignore, yet might learn to embrace and understand.

— Philippe Van Cauteren, La Fontaine-Saint-Martin, 9th of August, 2025

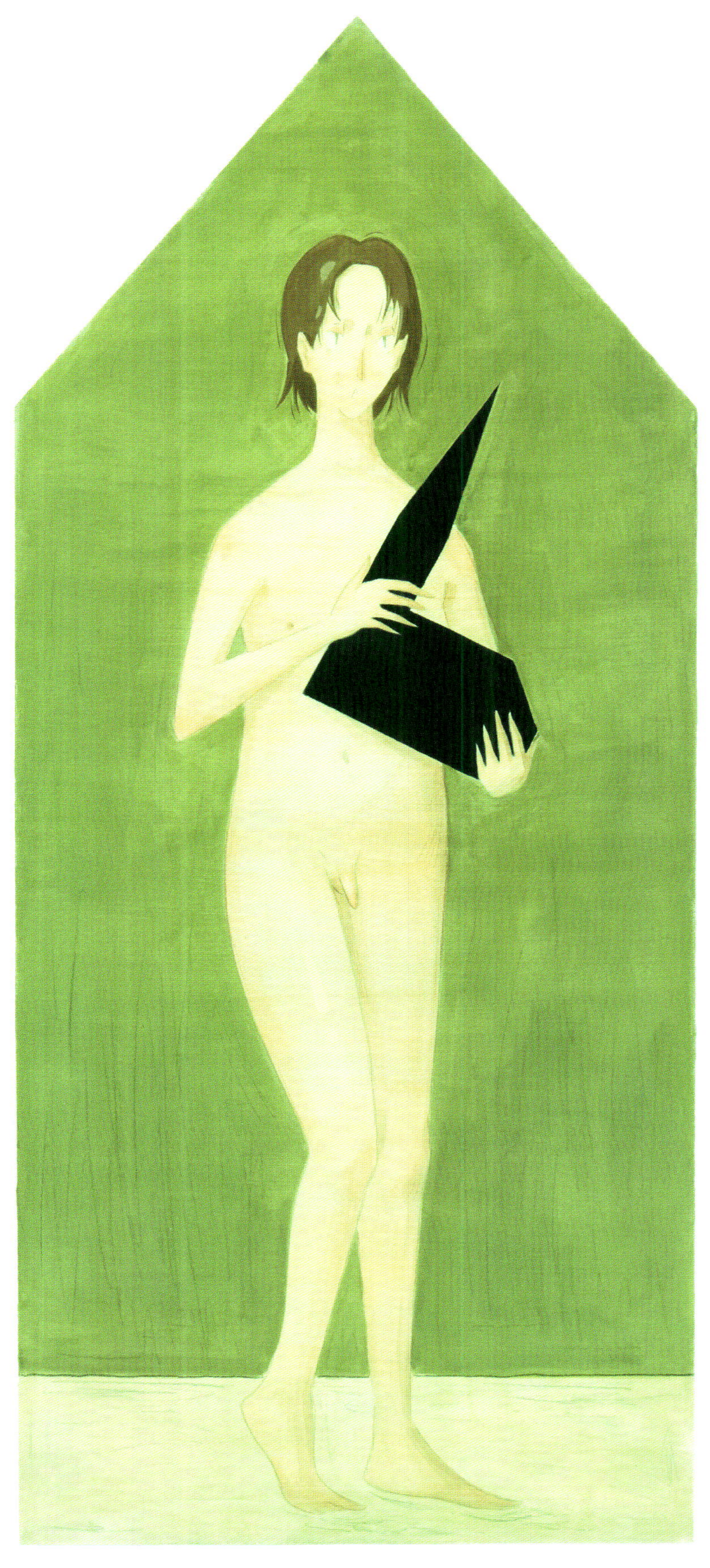

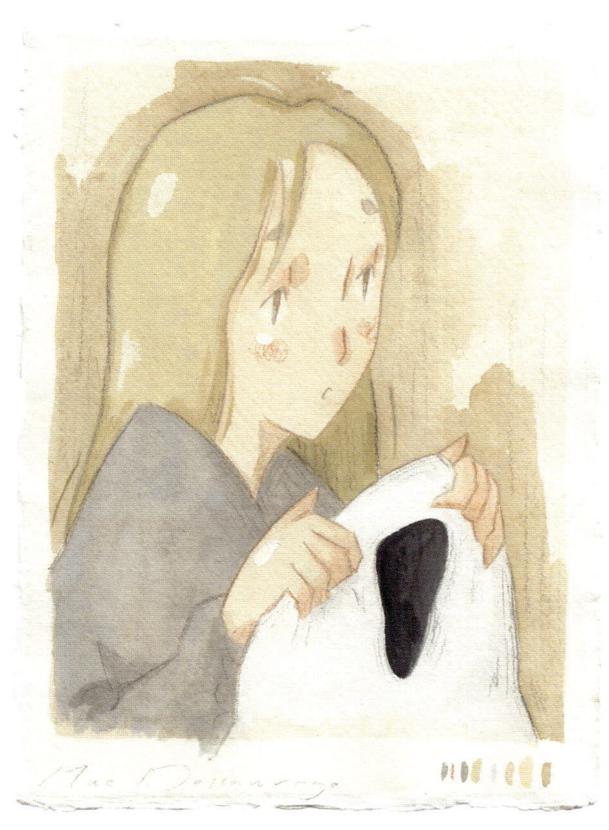

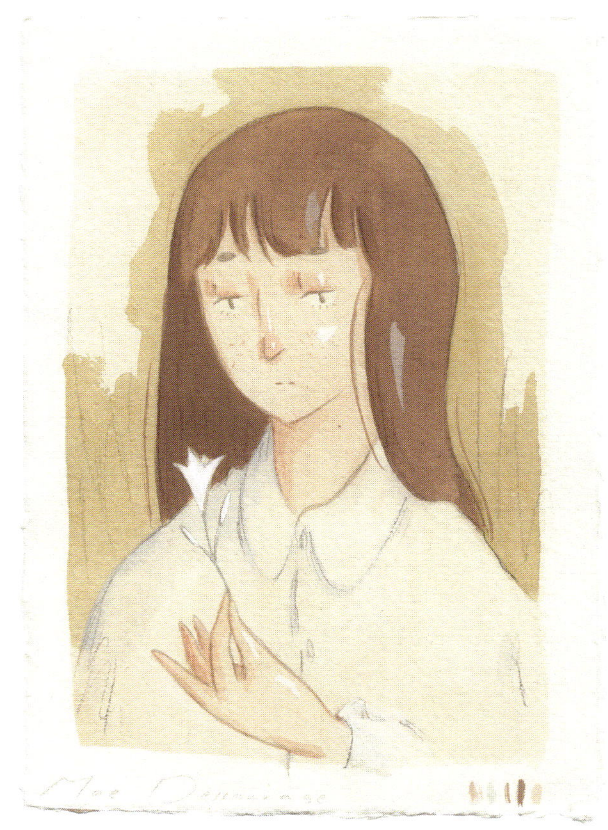

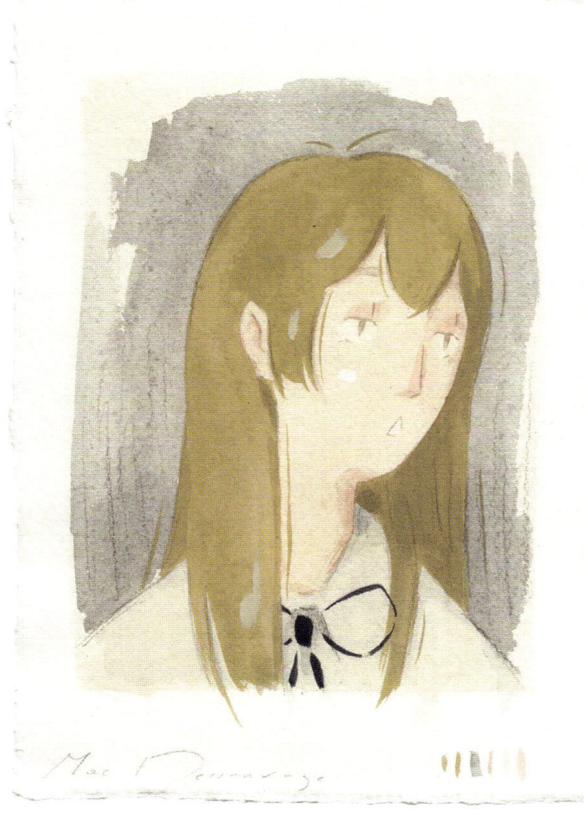

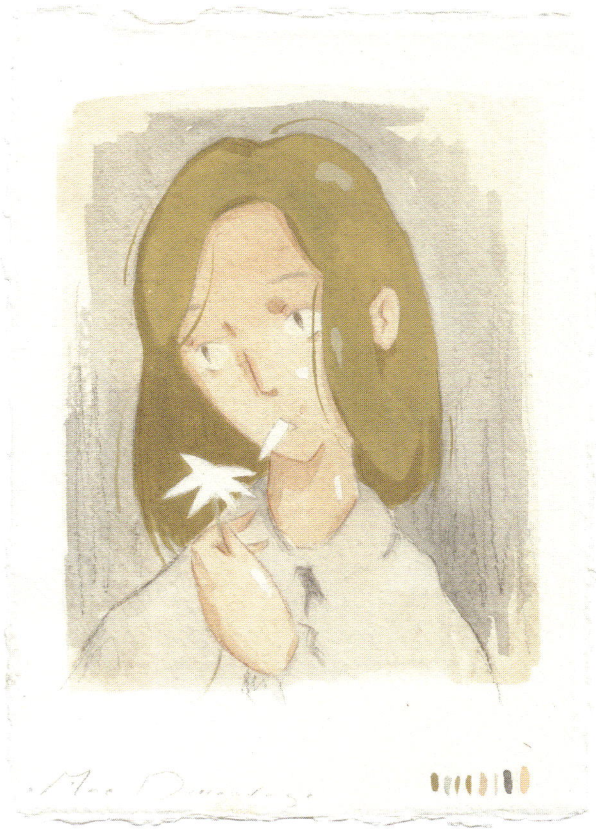

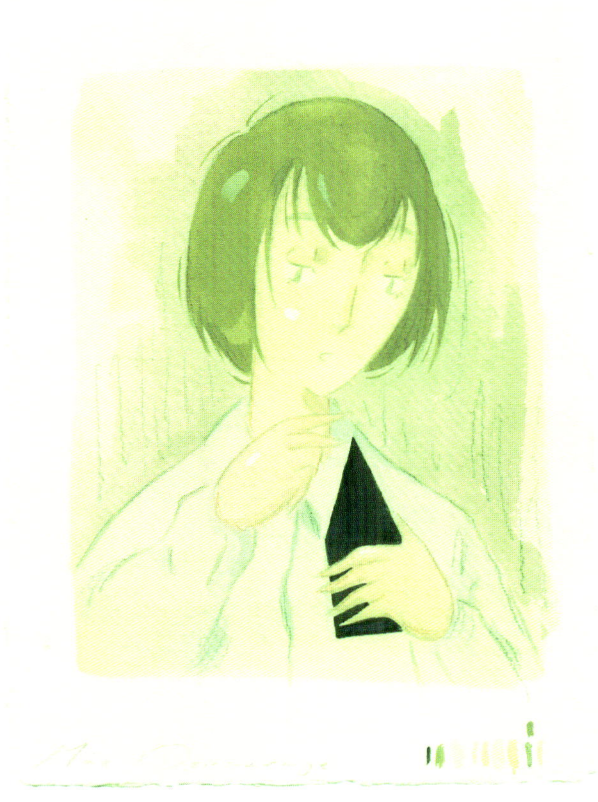

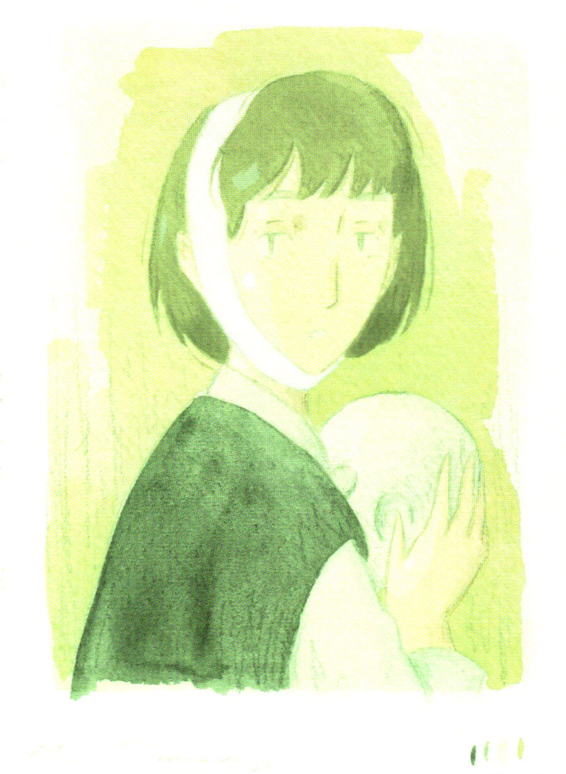

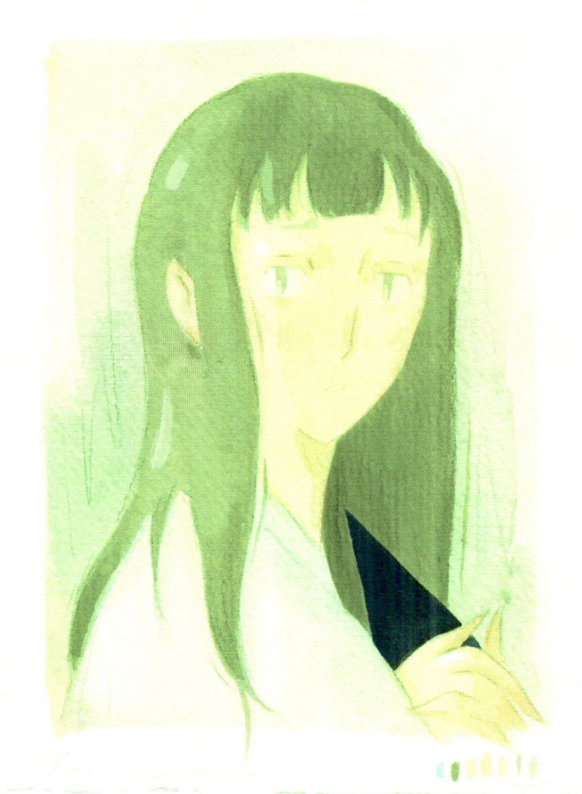

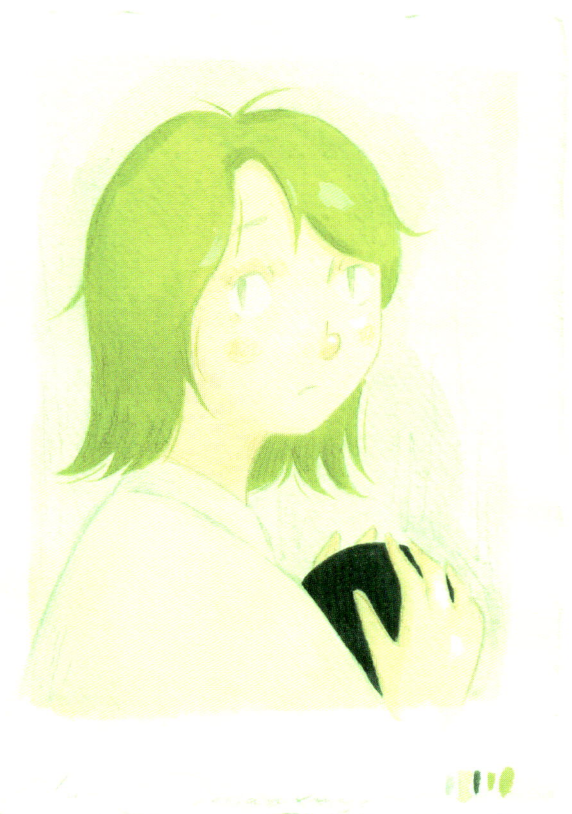

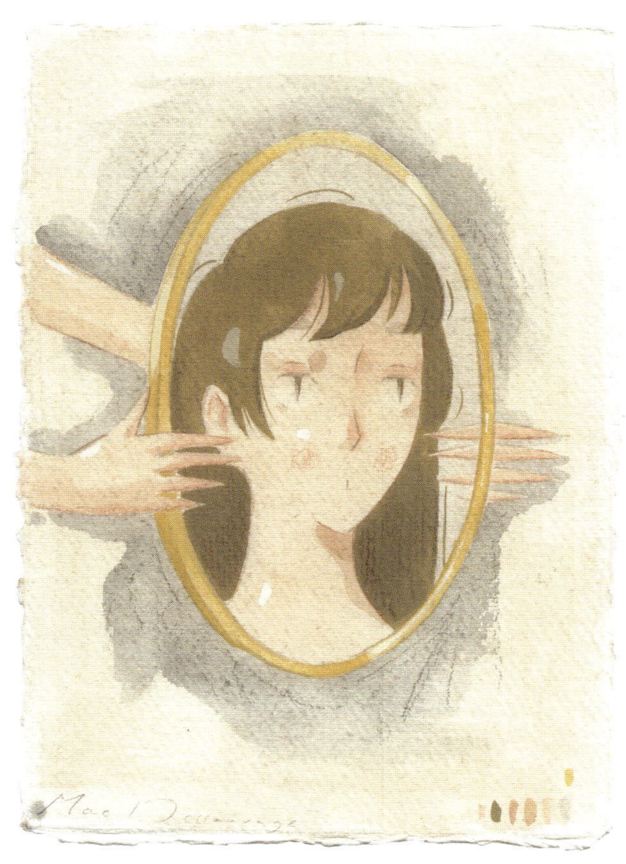
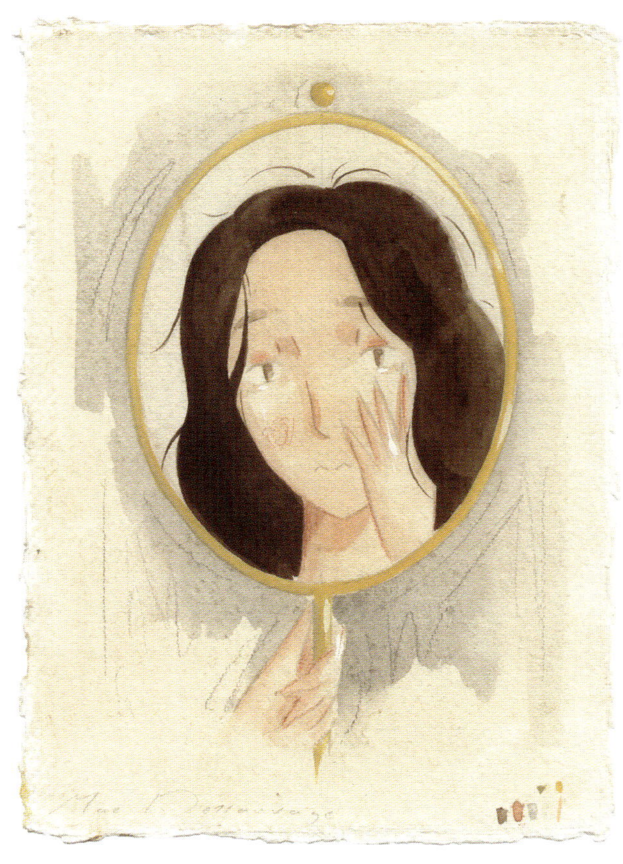
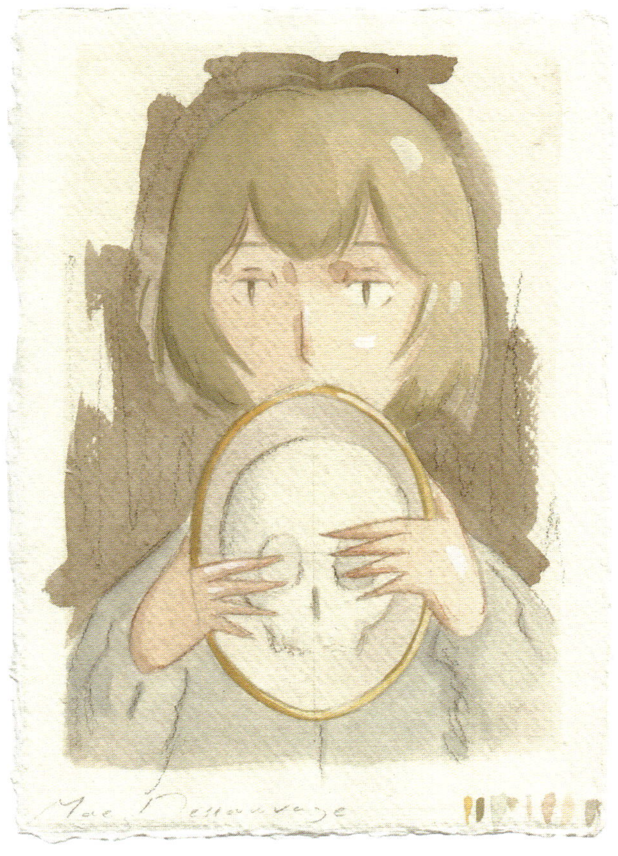
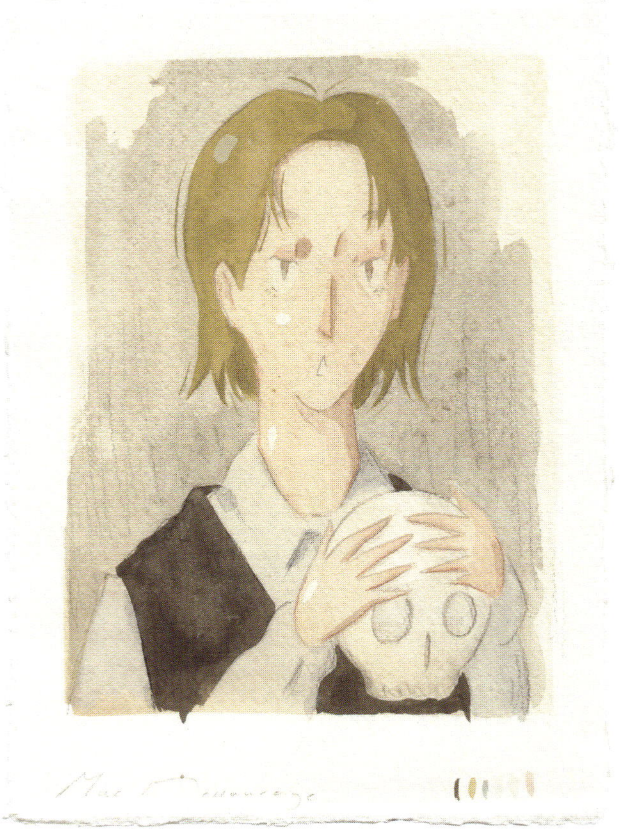

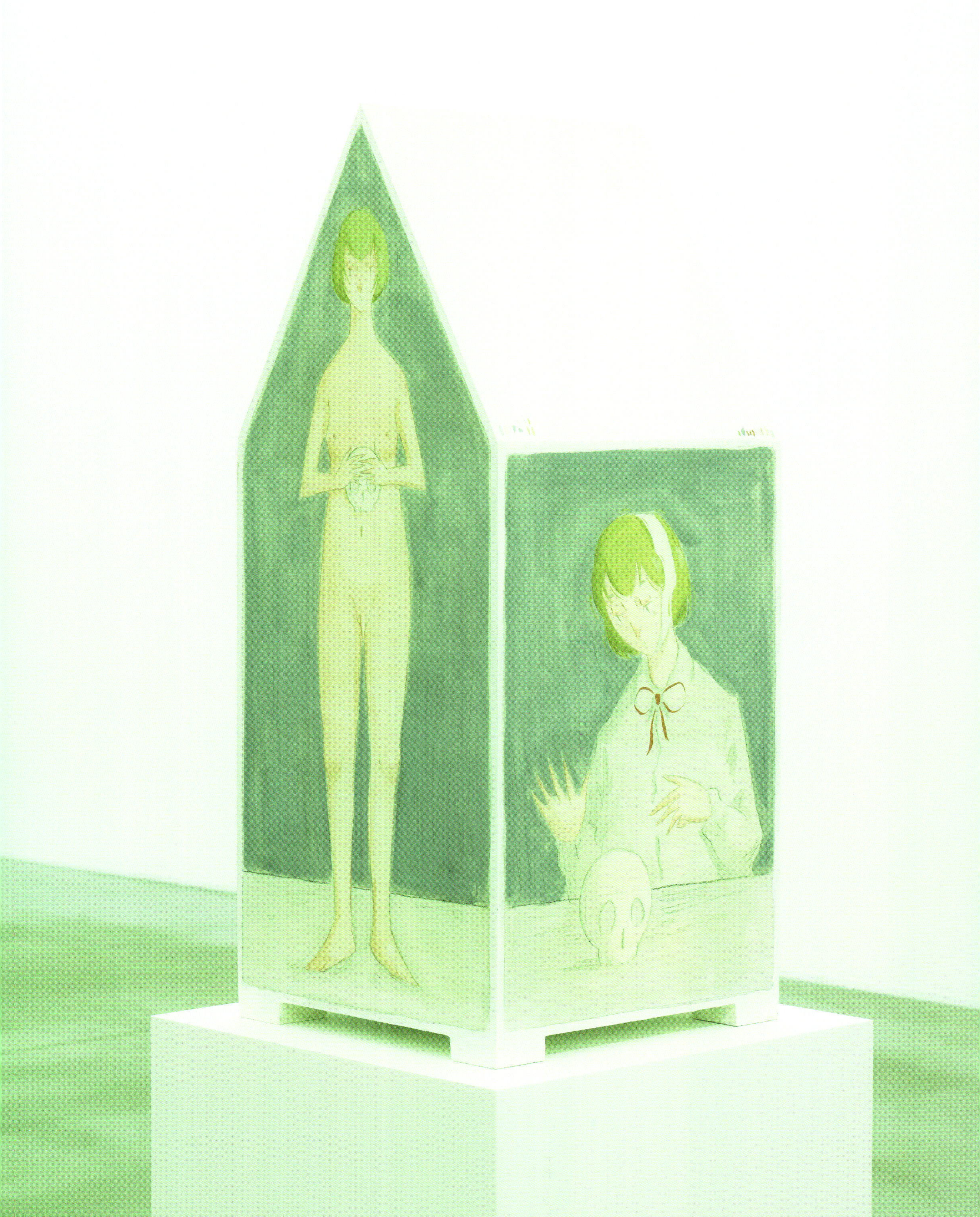

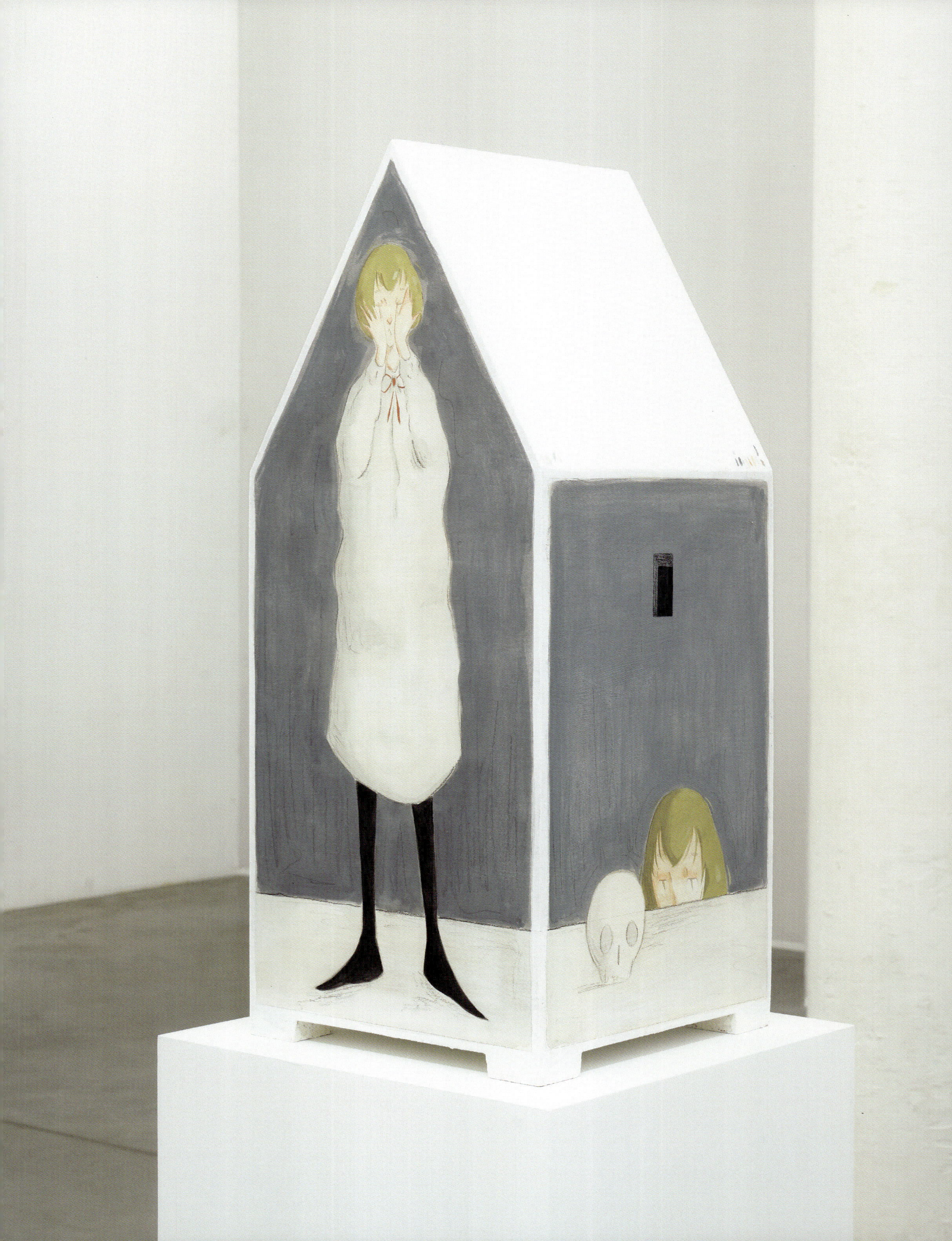

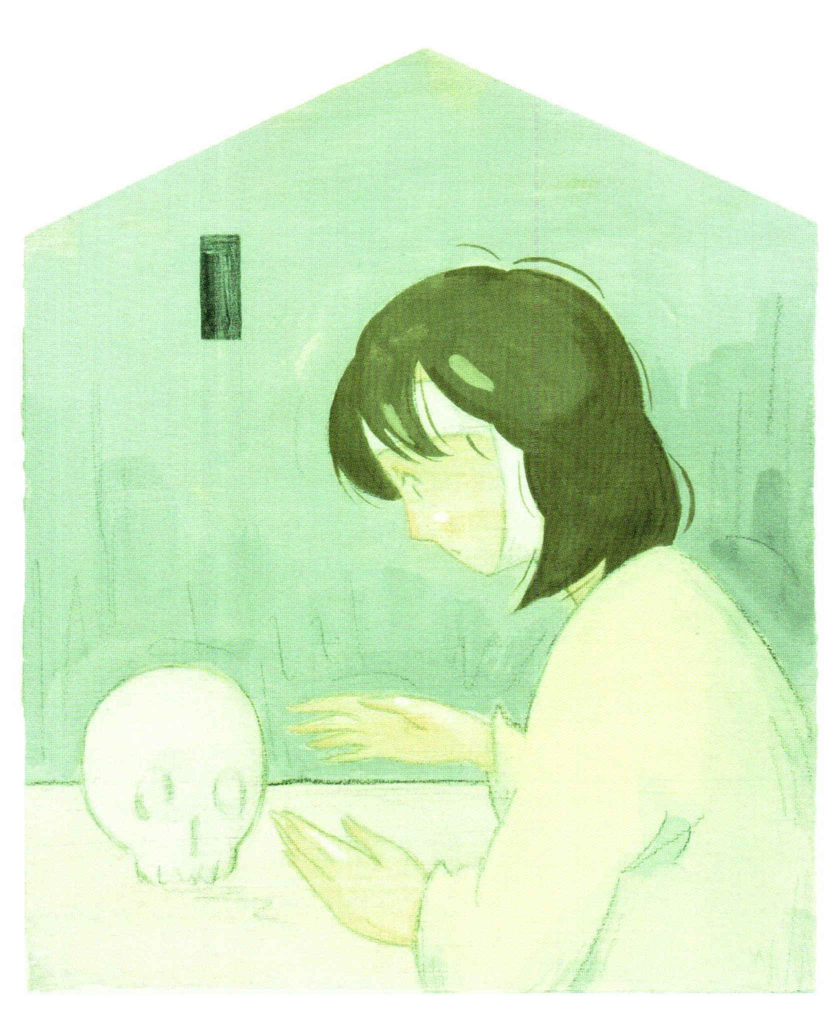

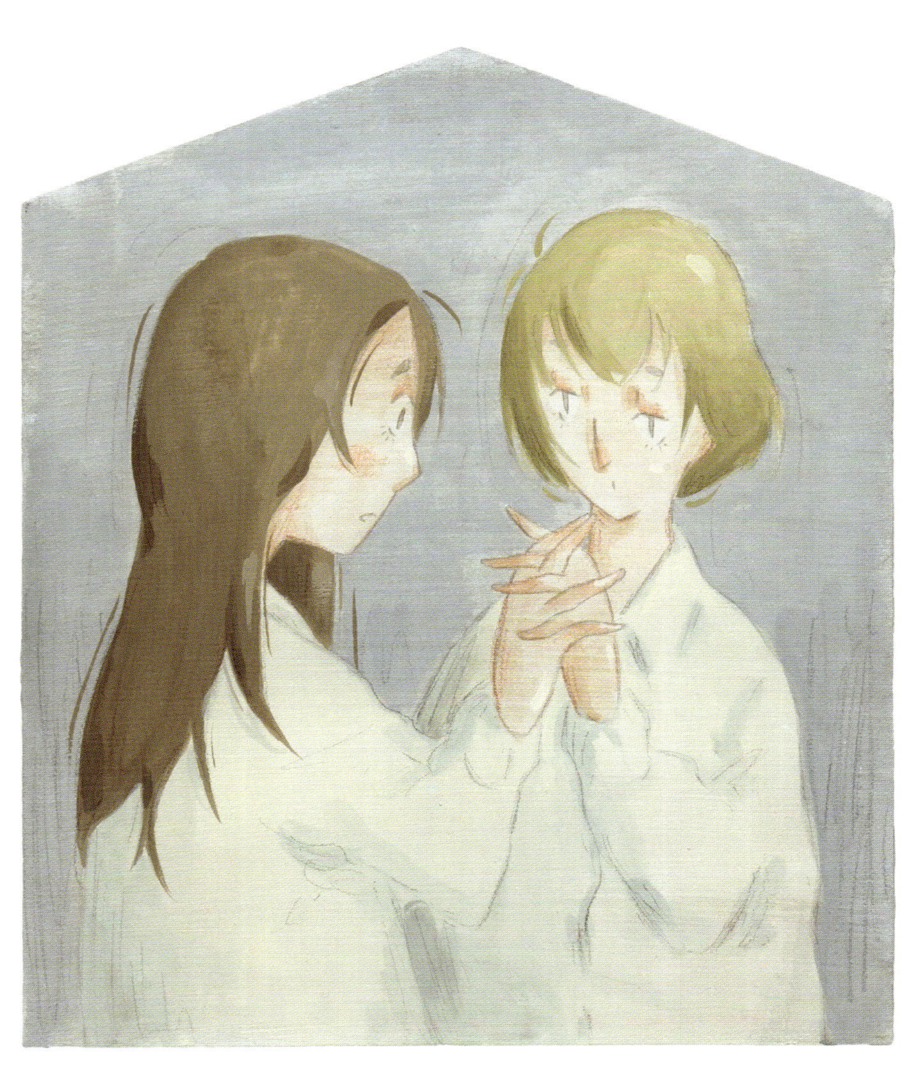

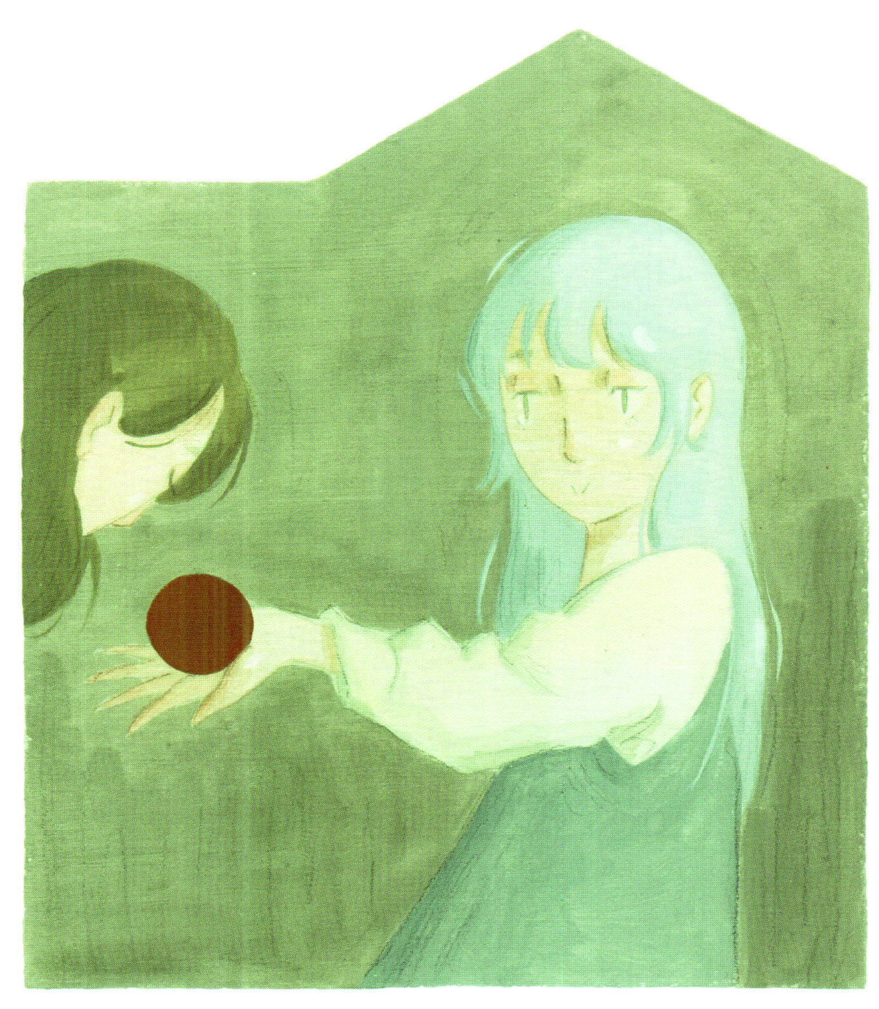

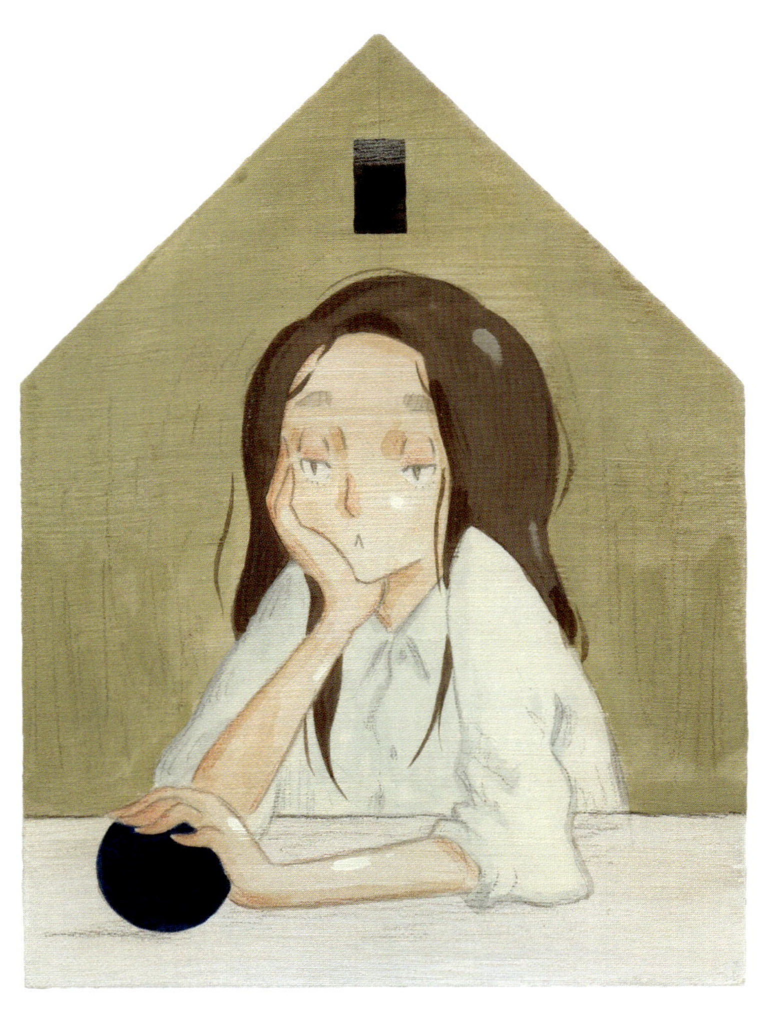

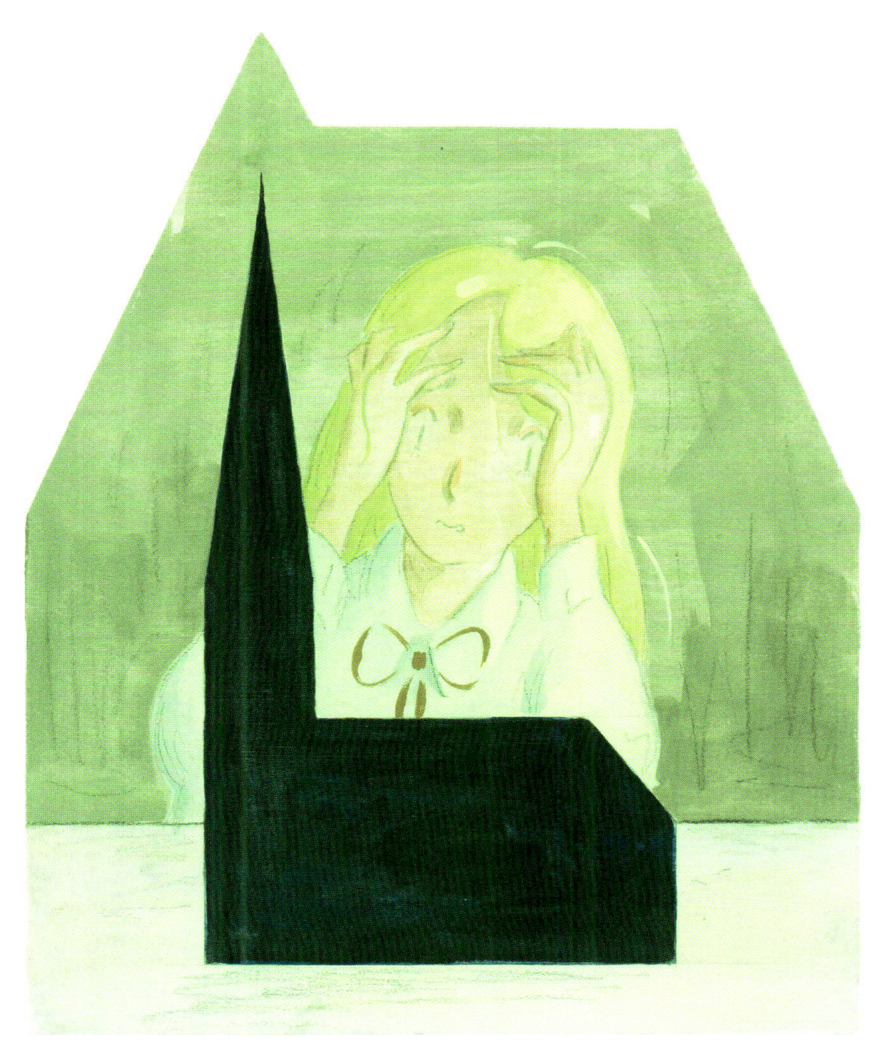

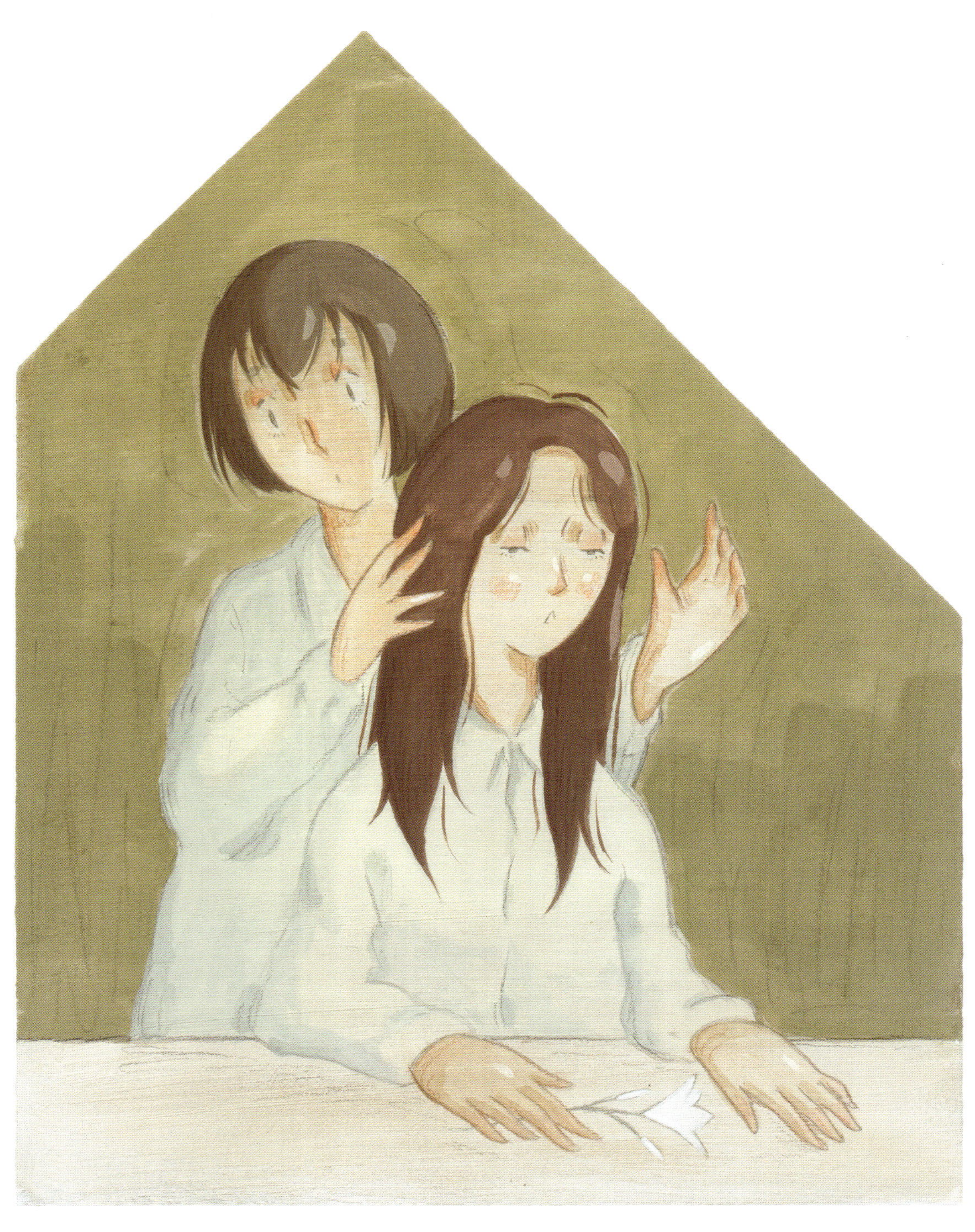

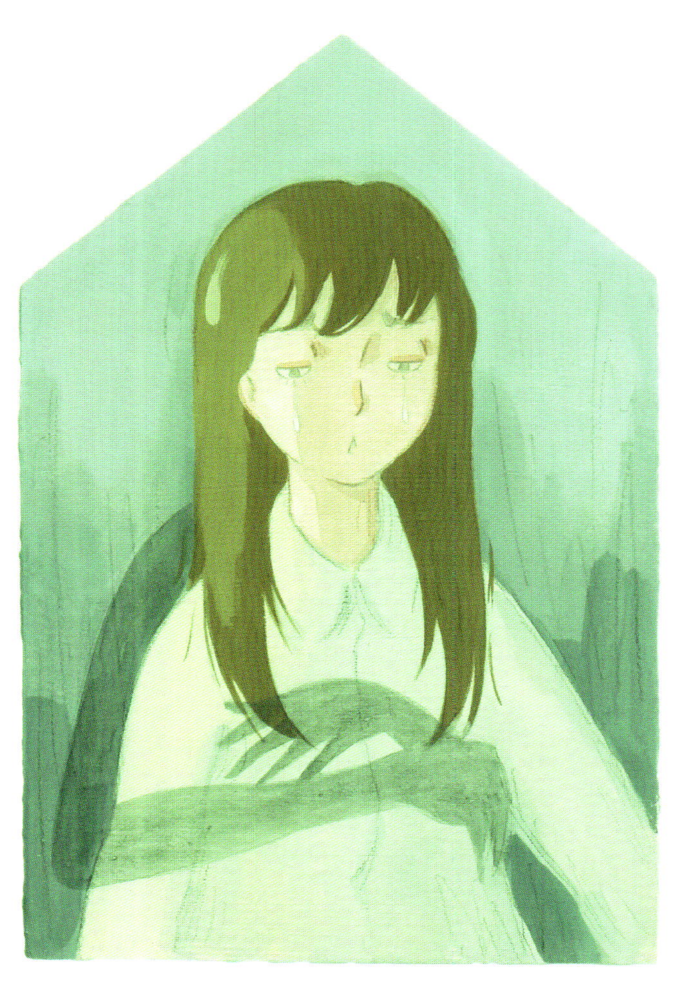

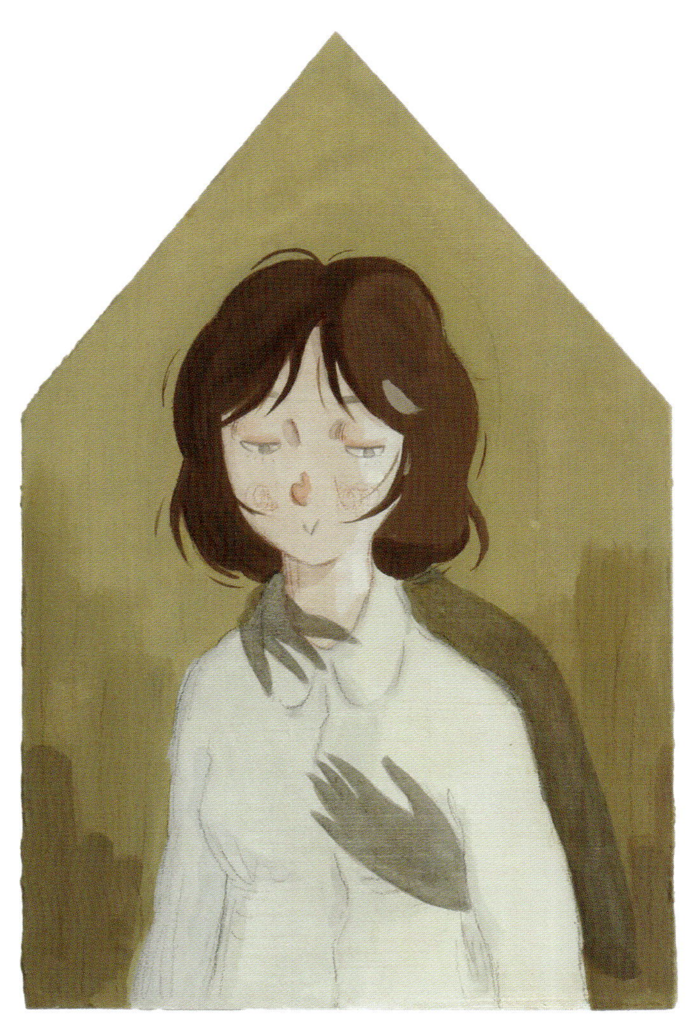

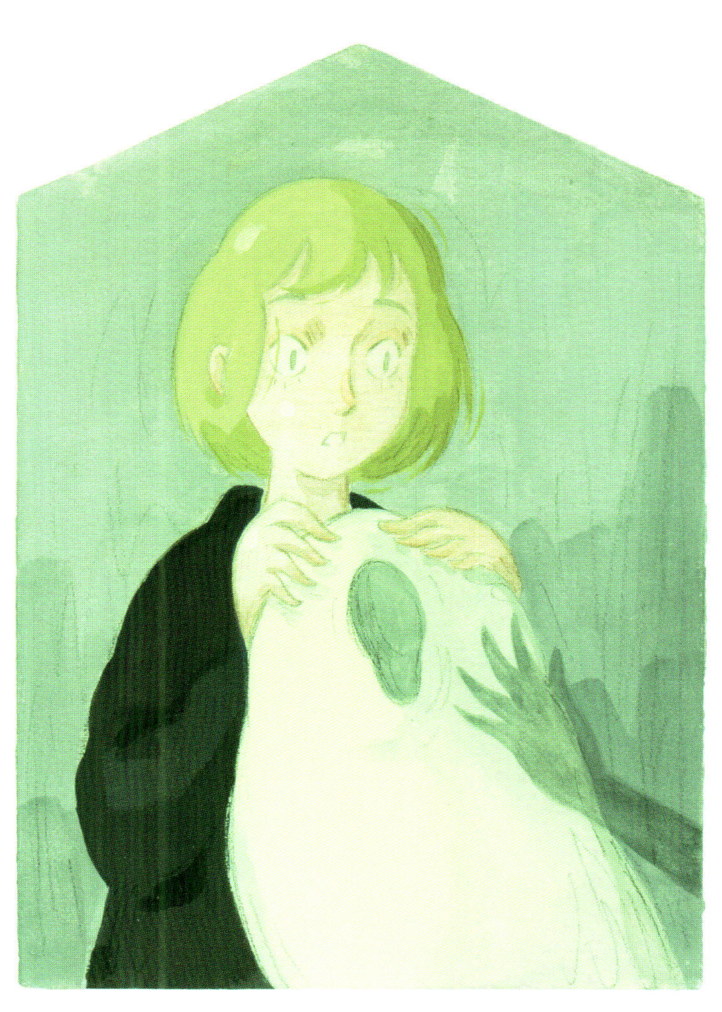

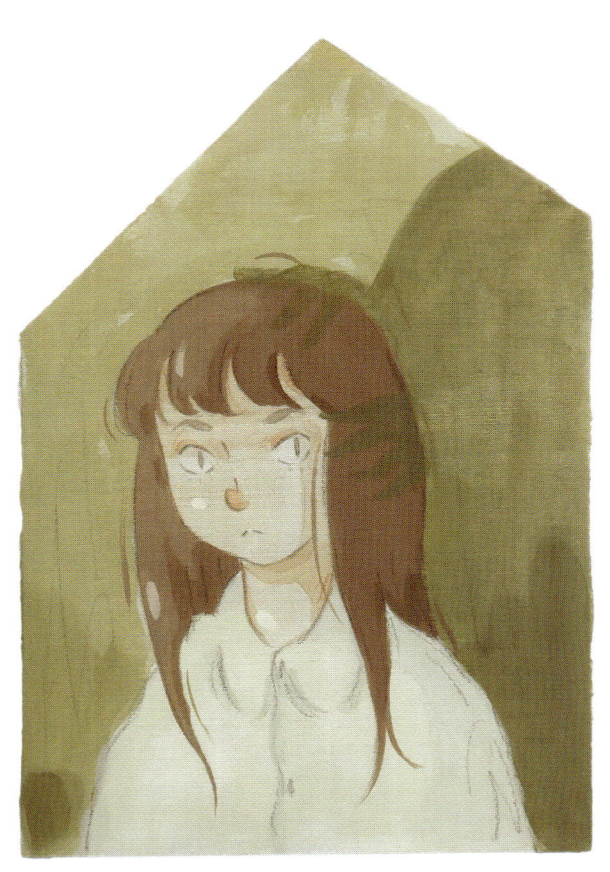

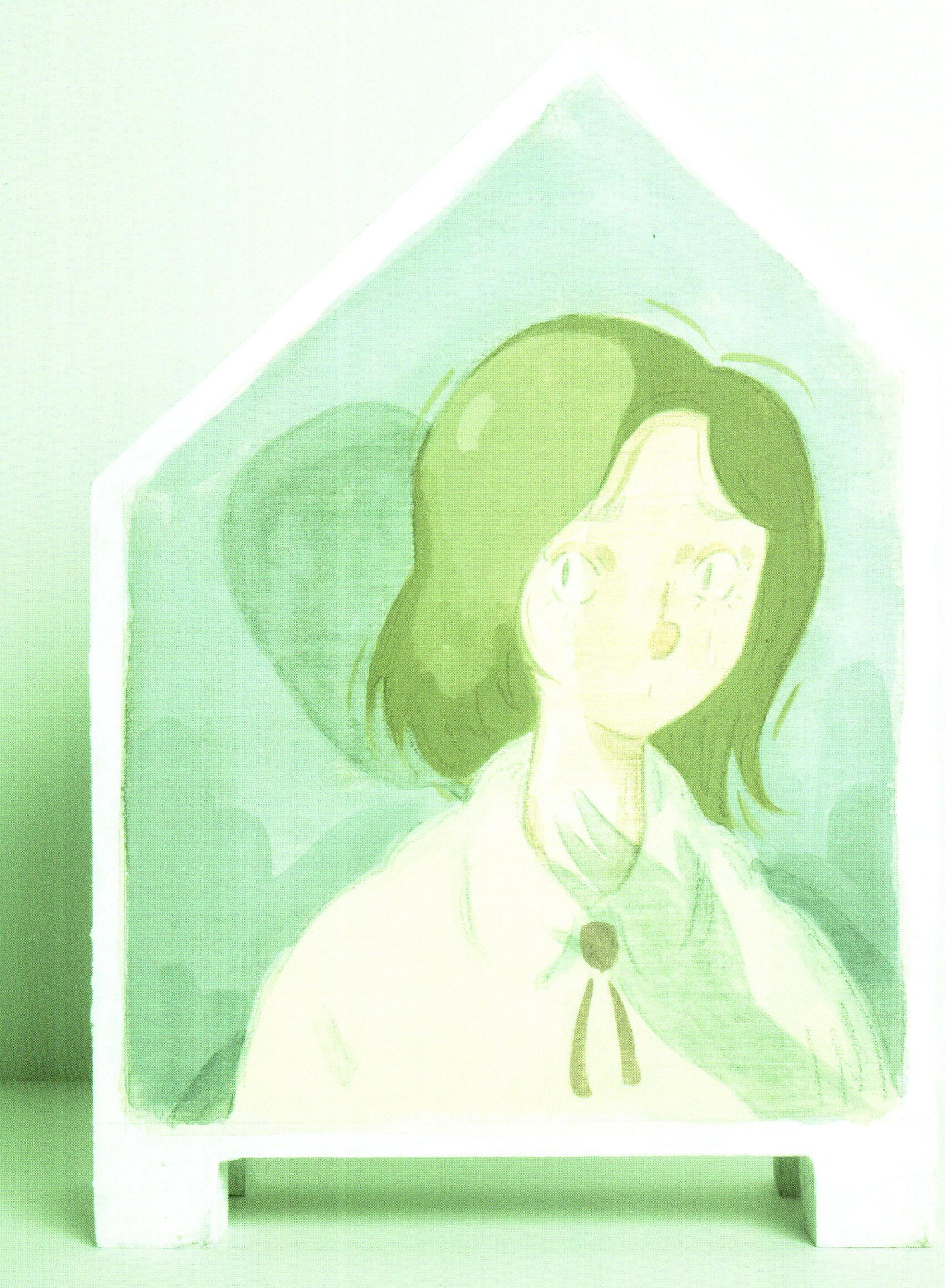

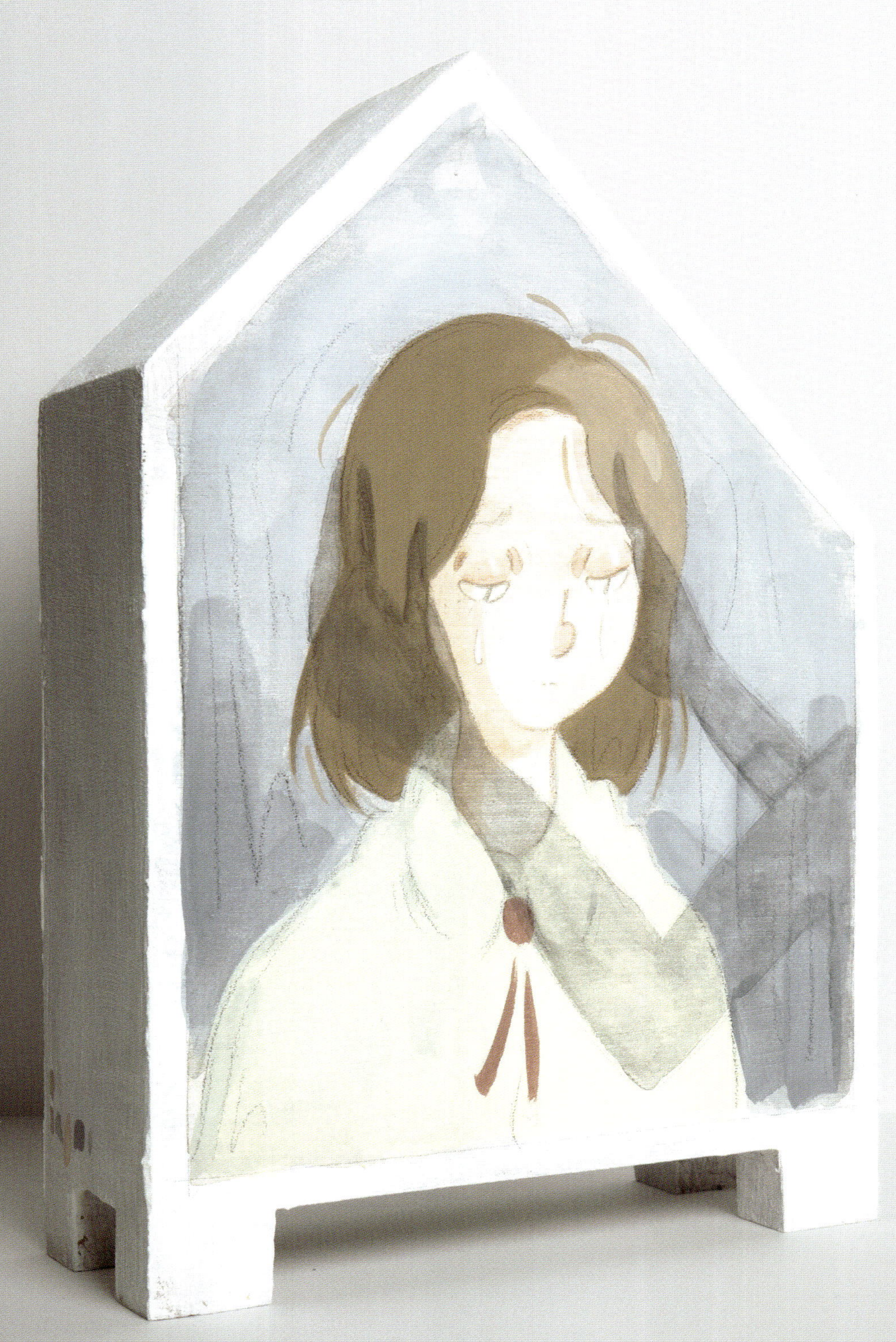

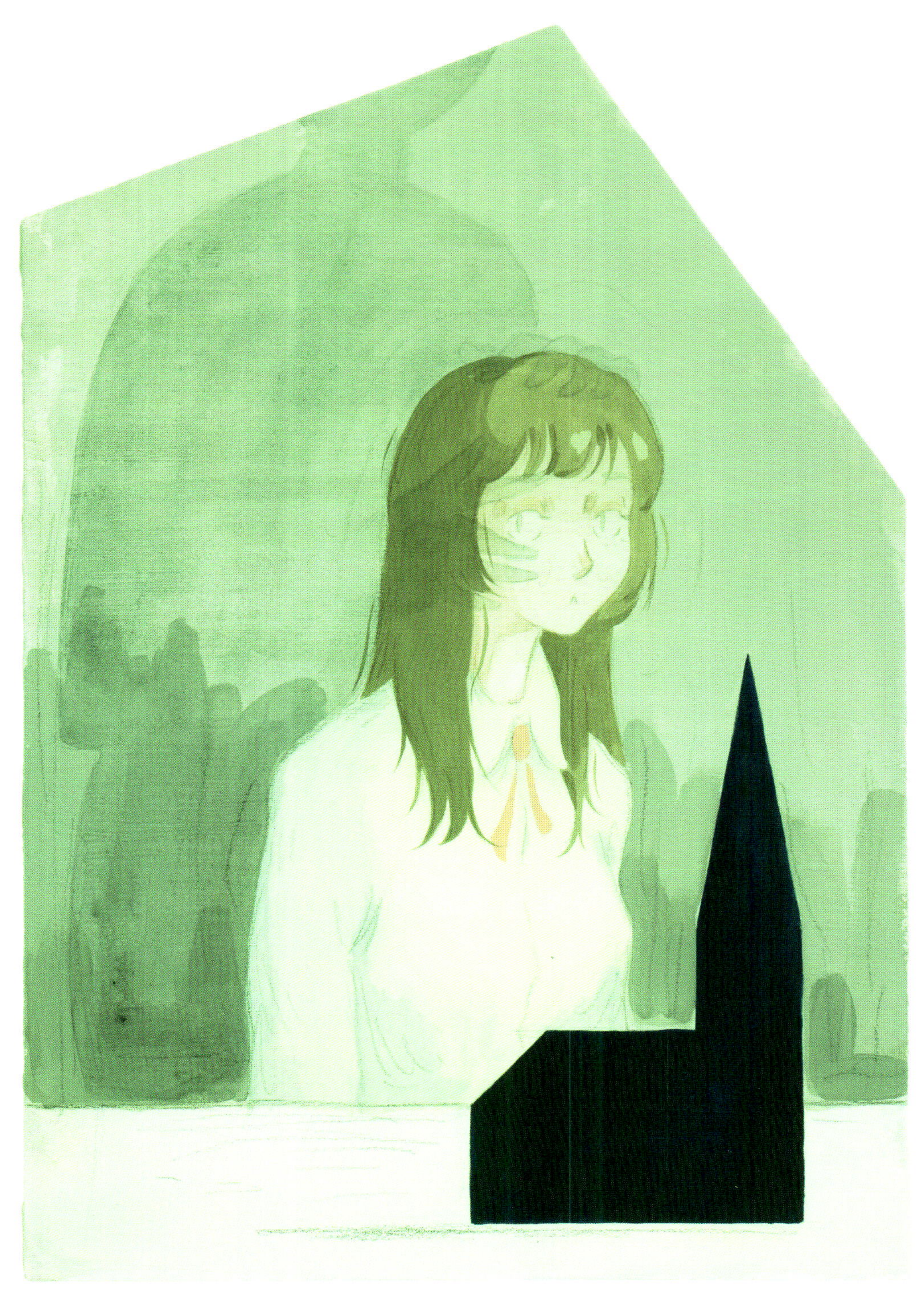

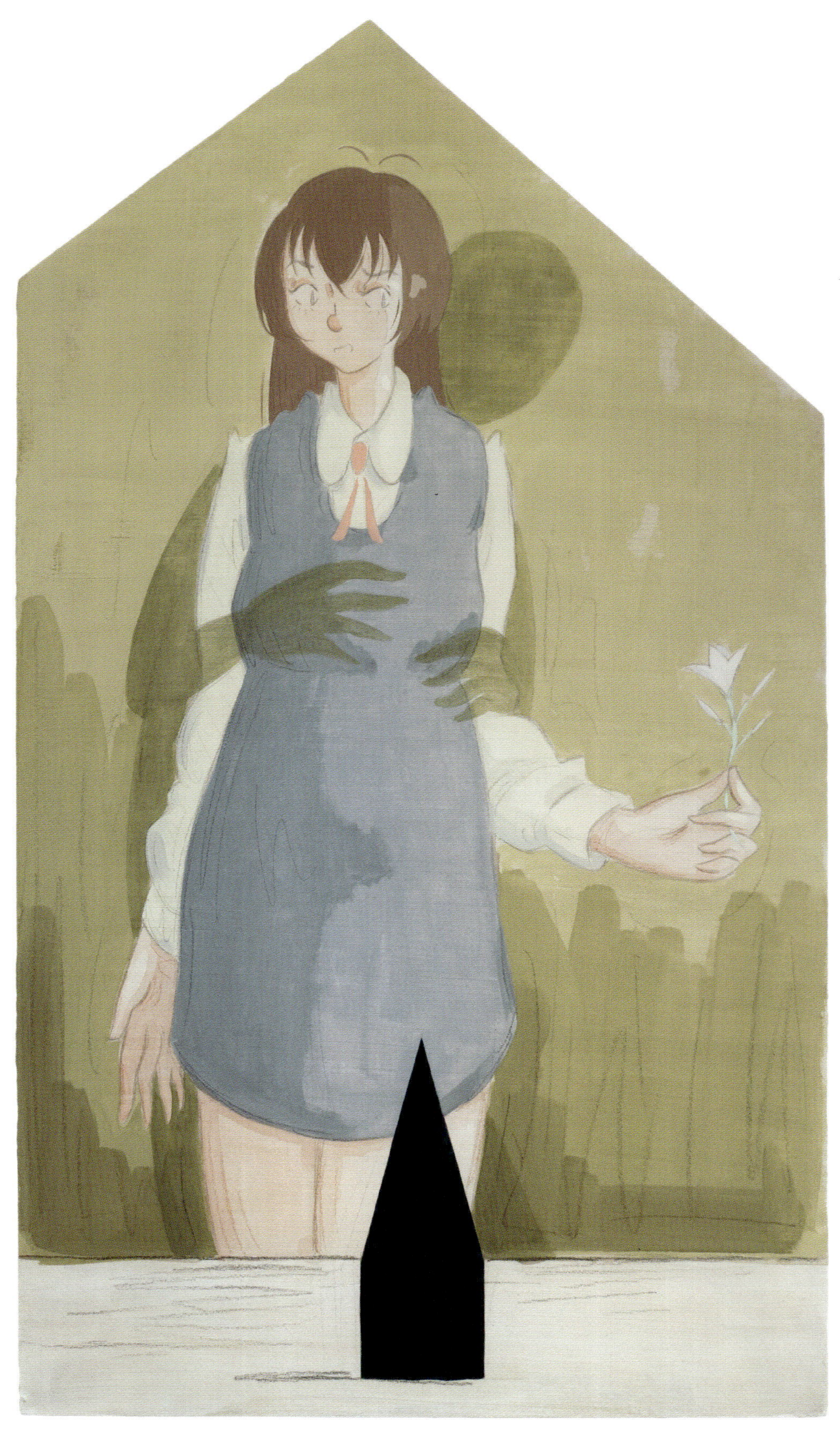

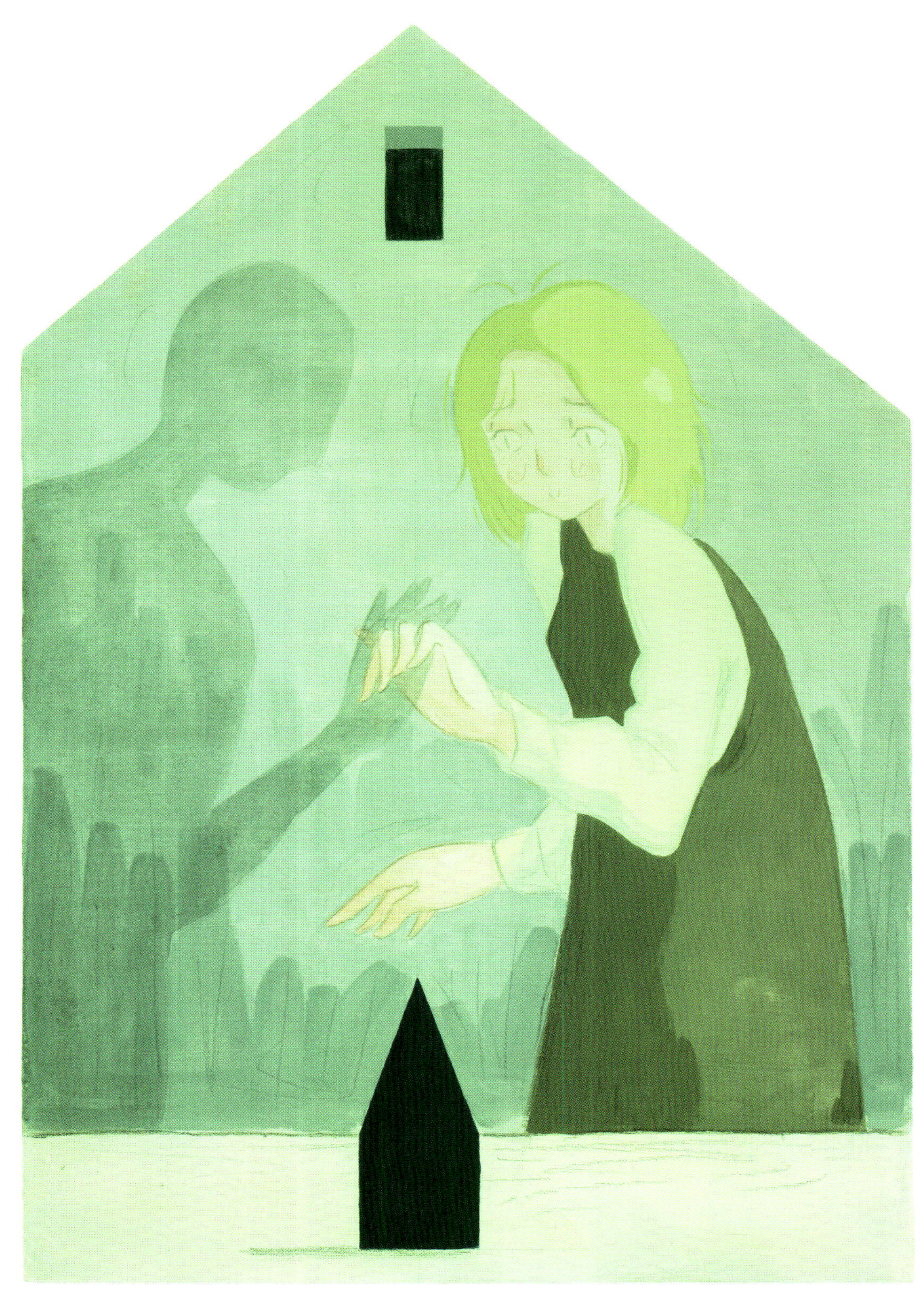

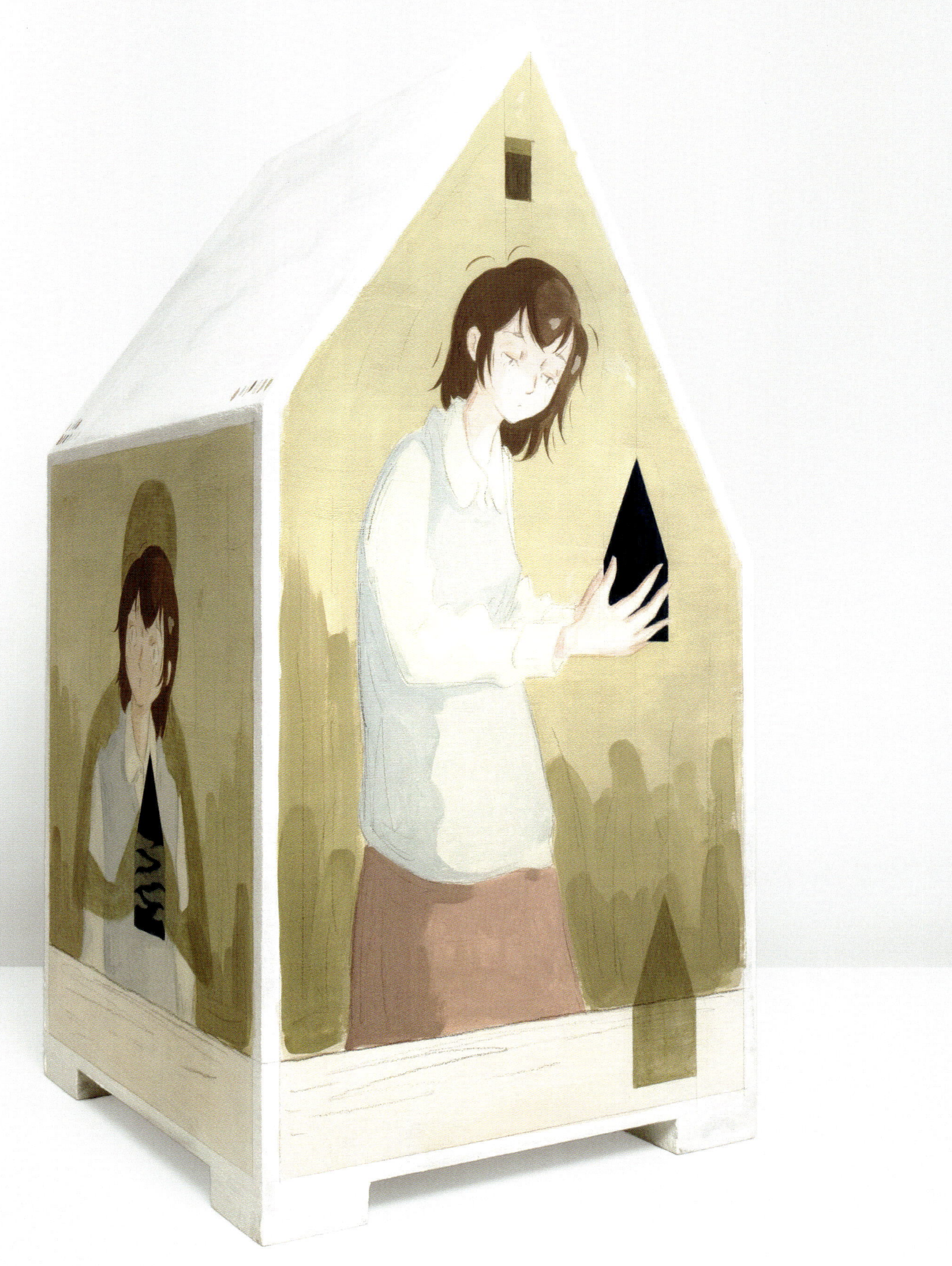

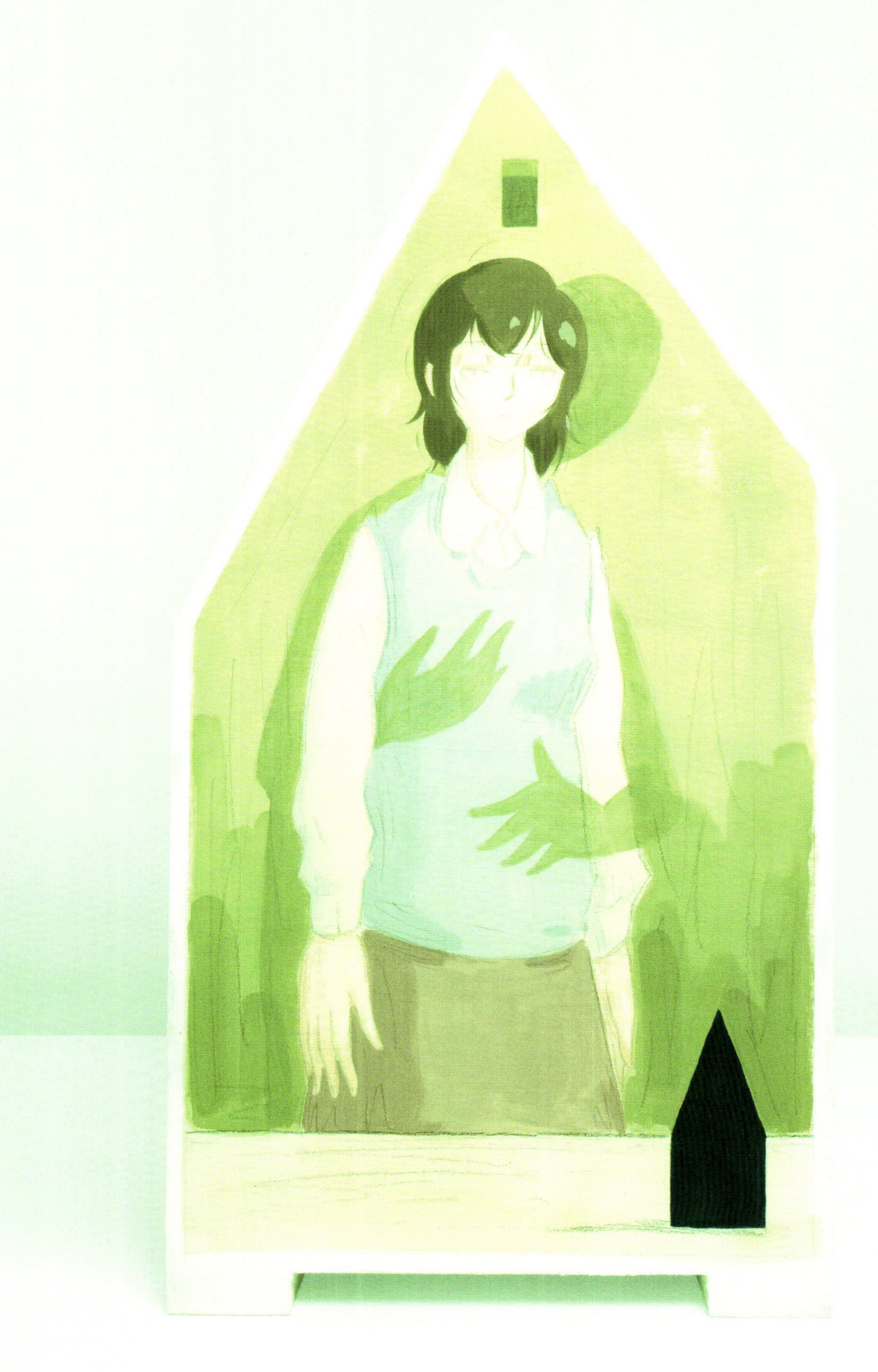

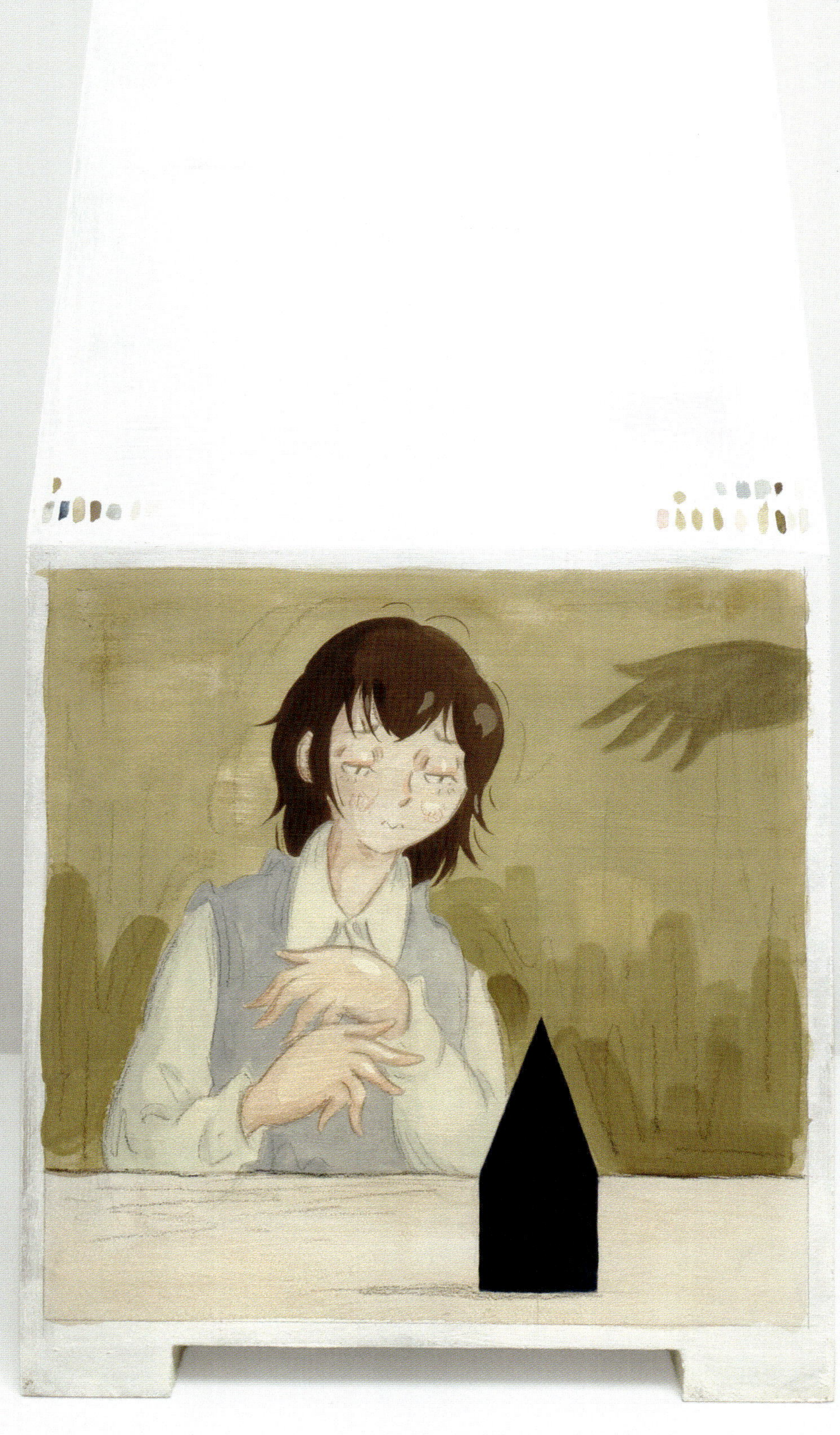

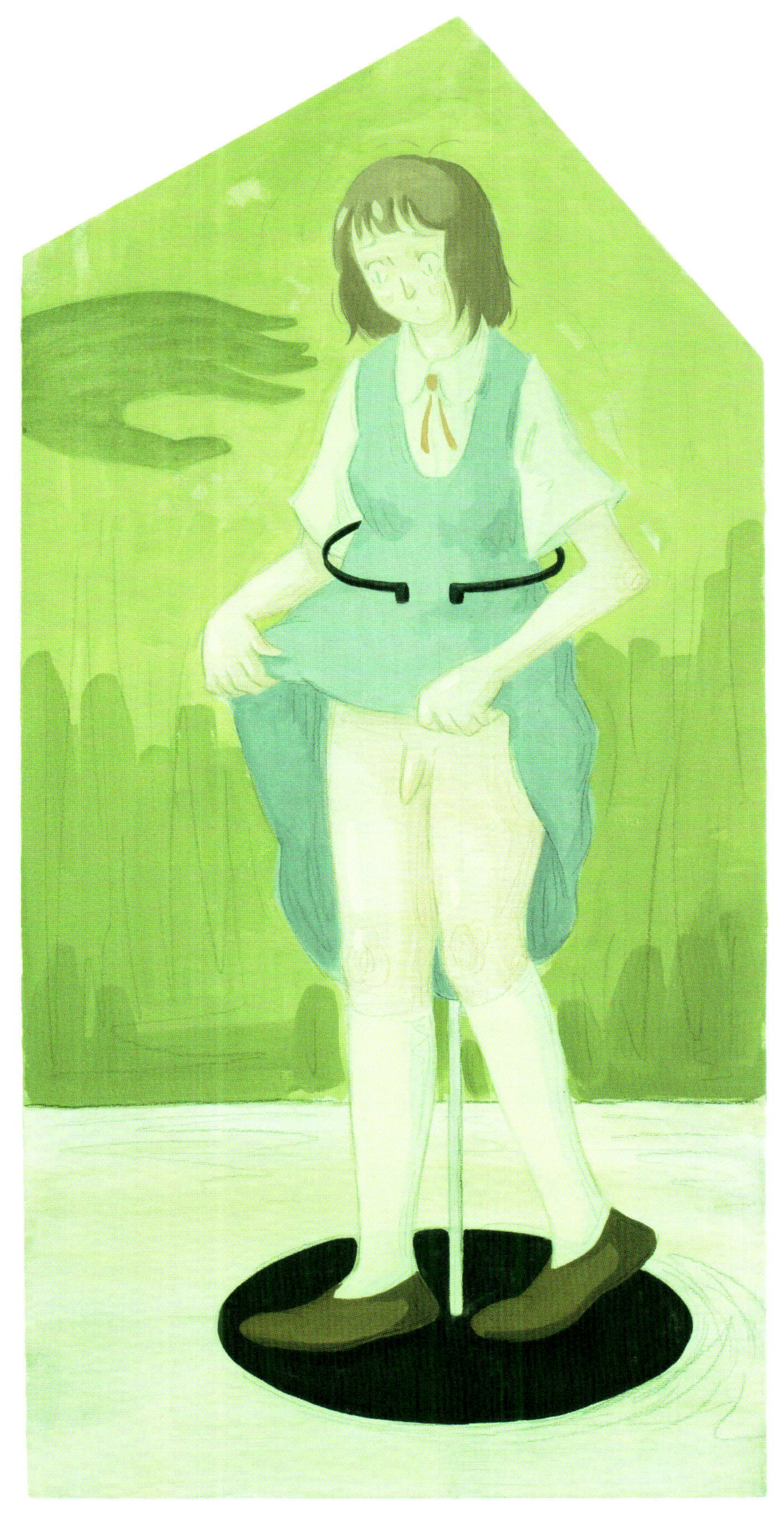

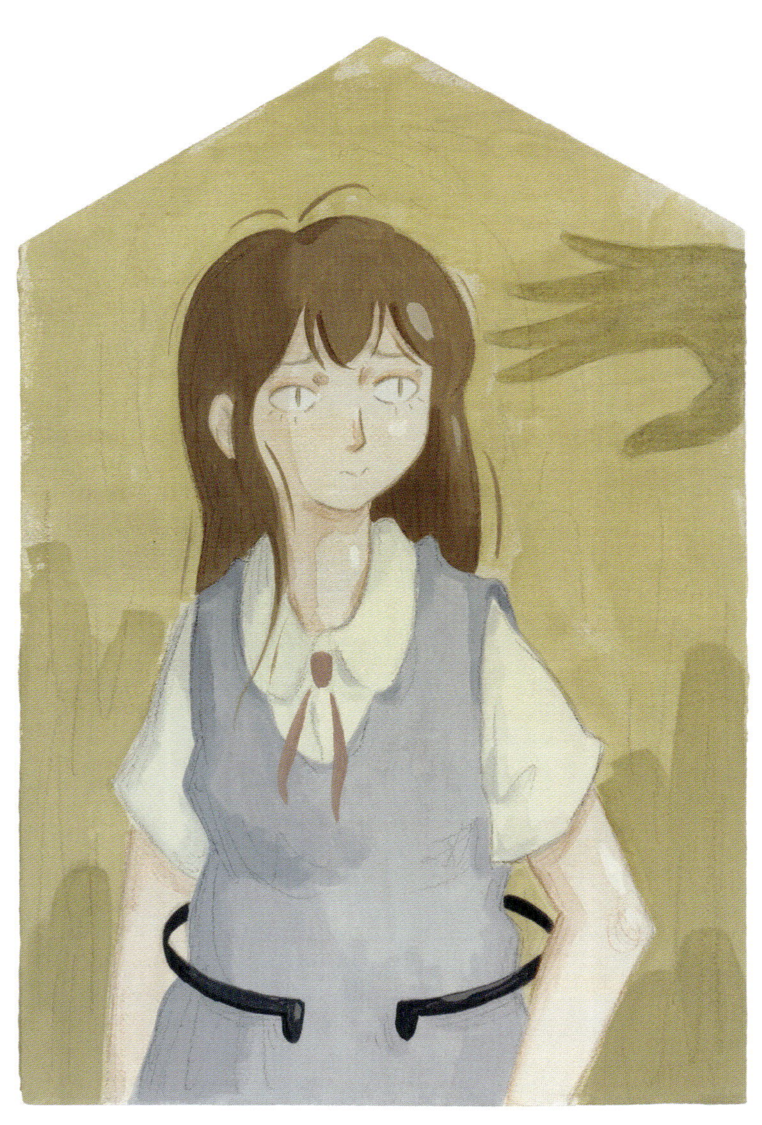

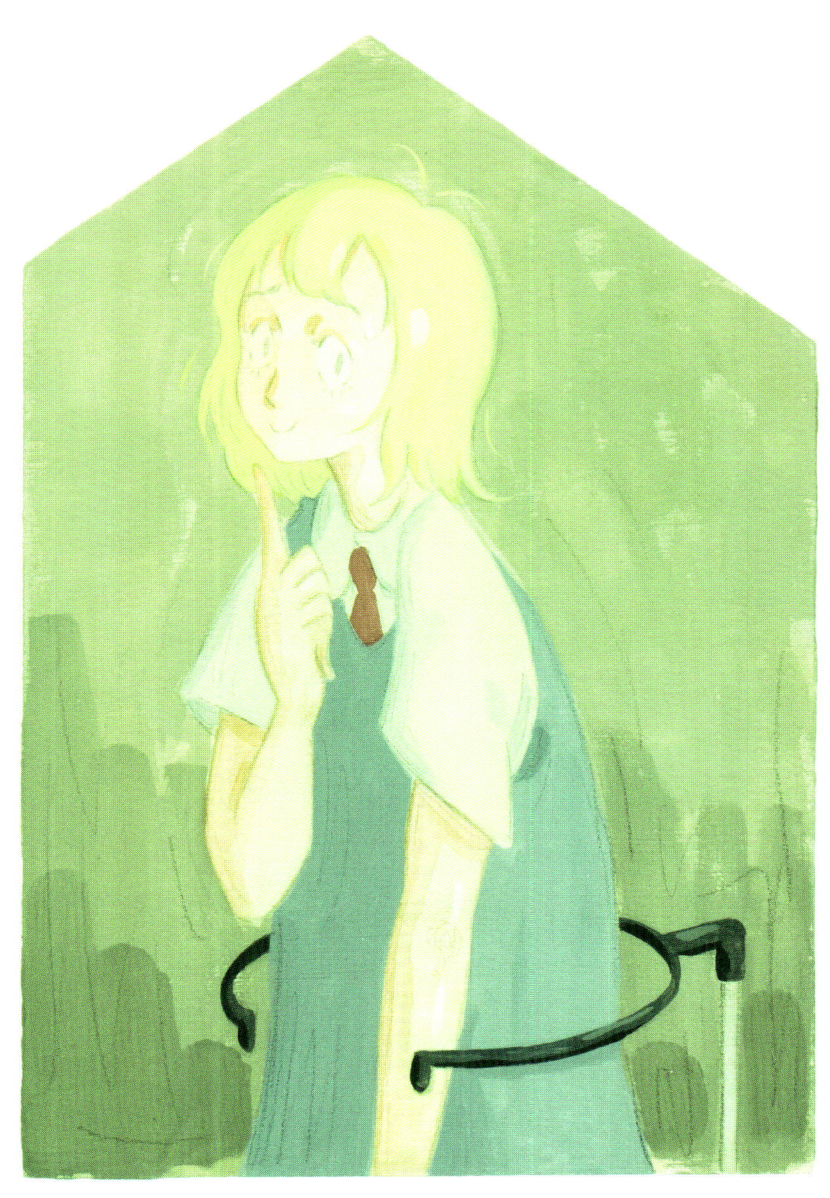

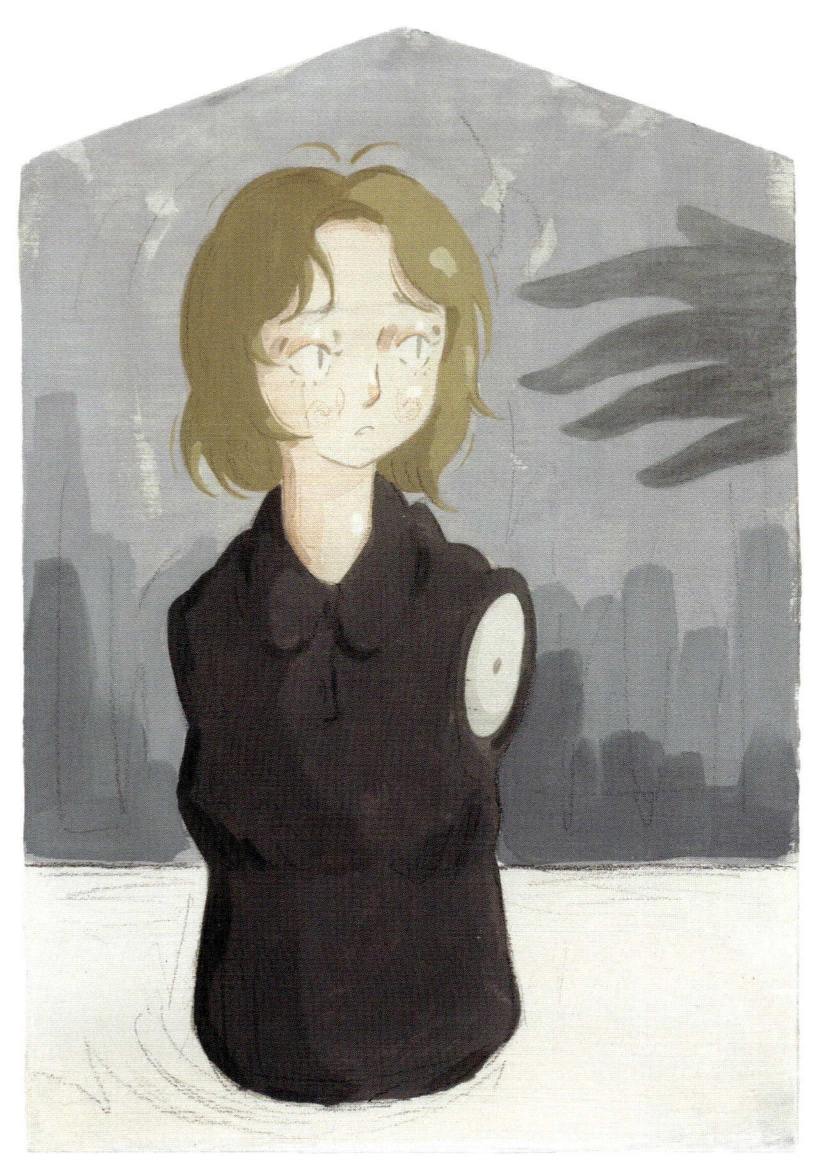

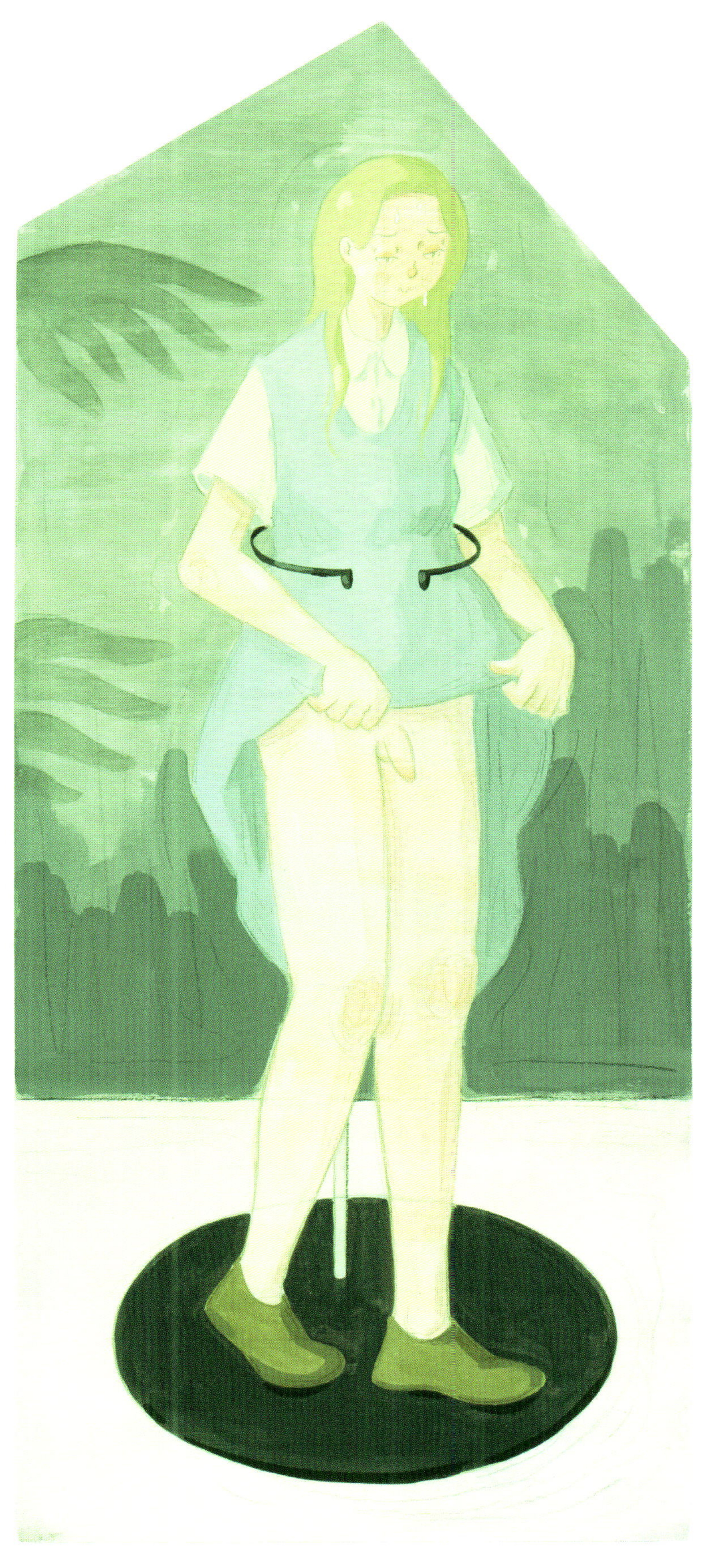

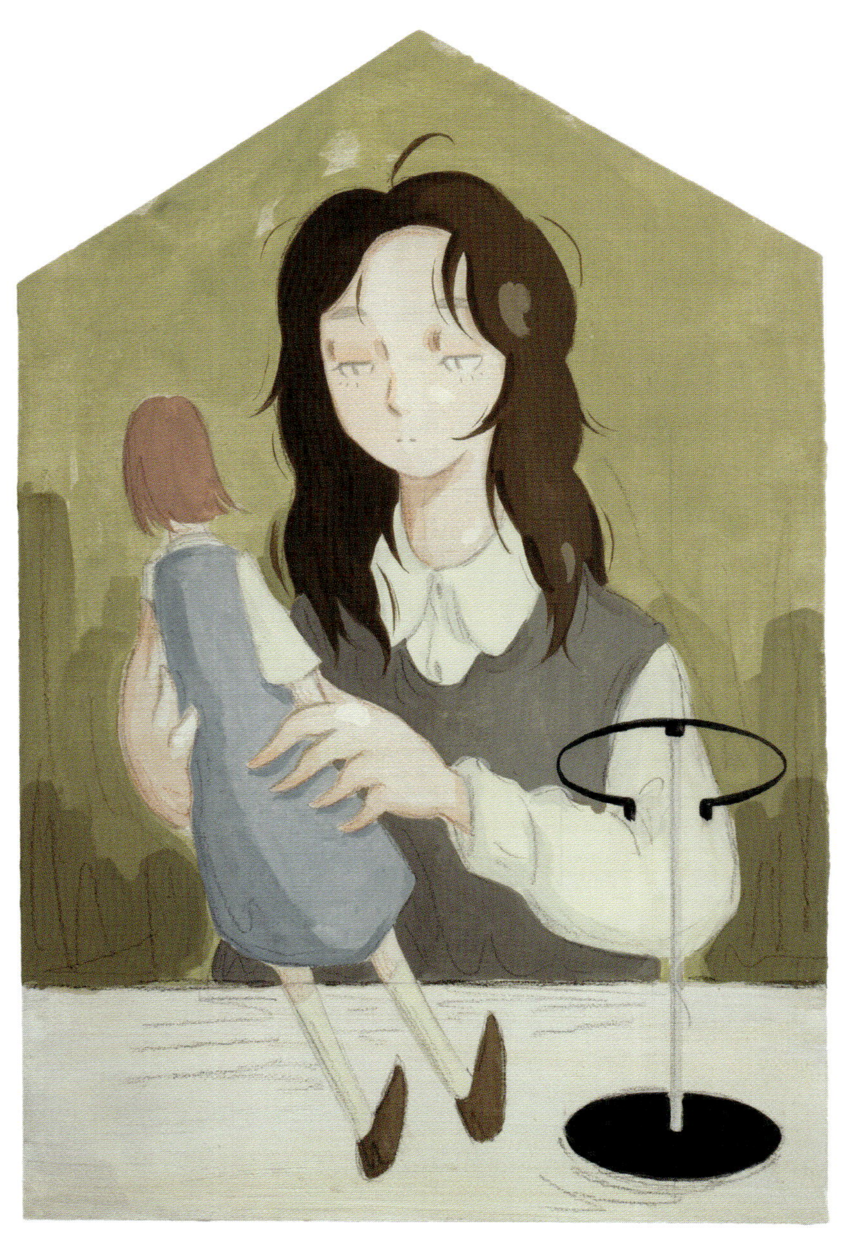

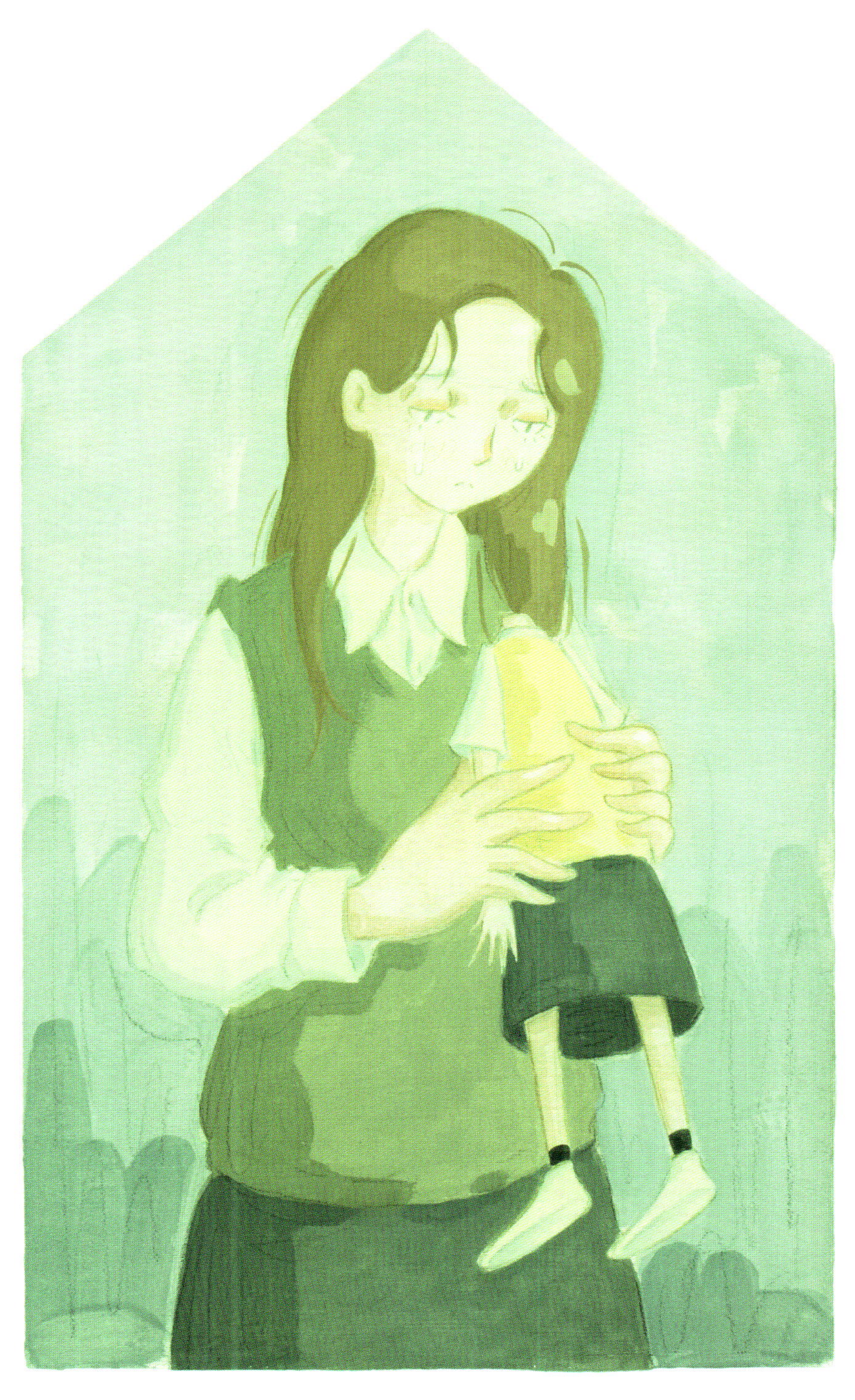

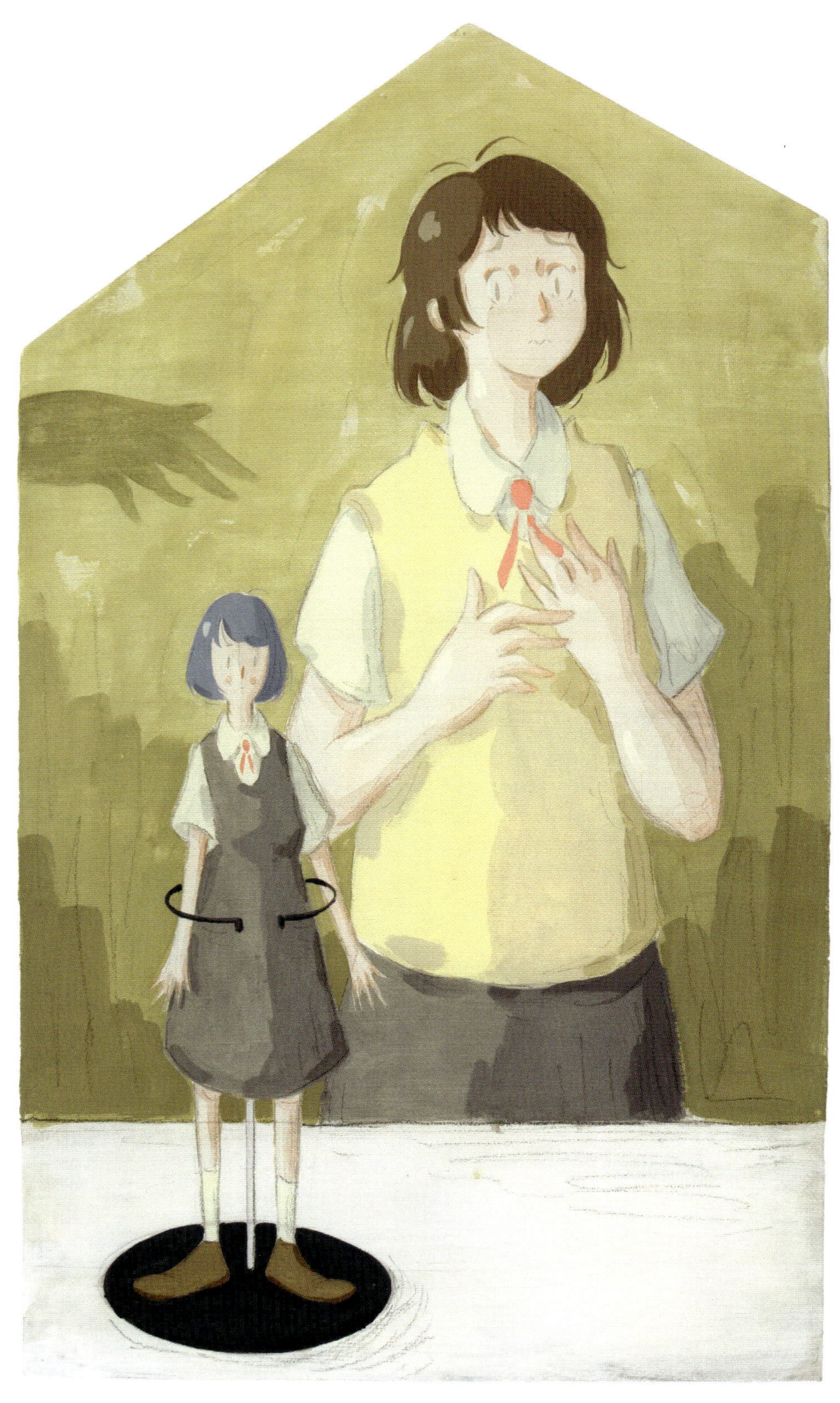

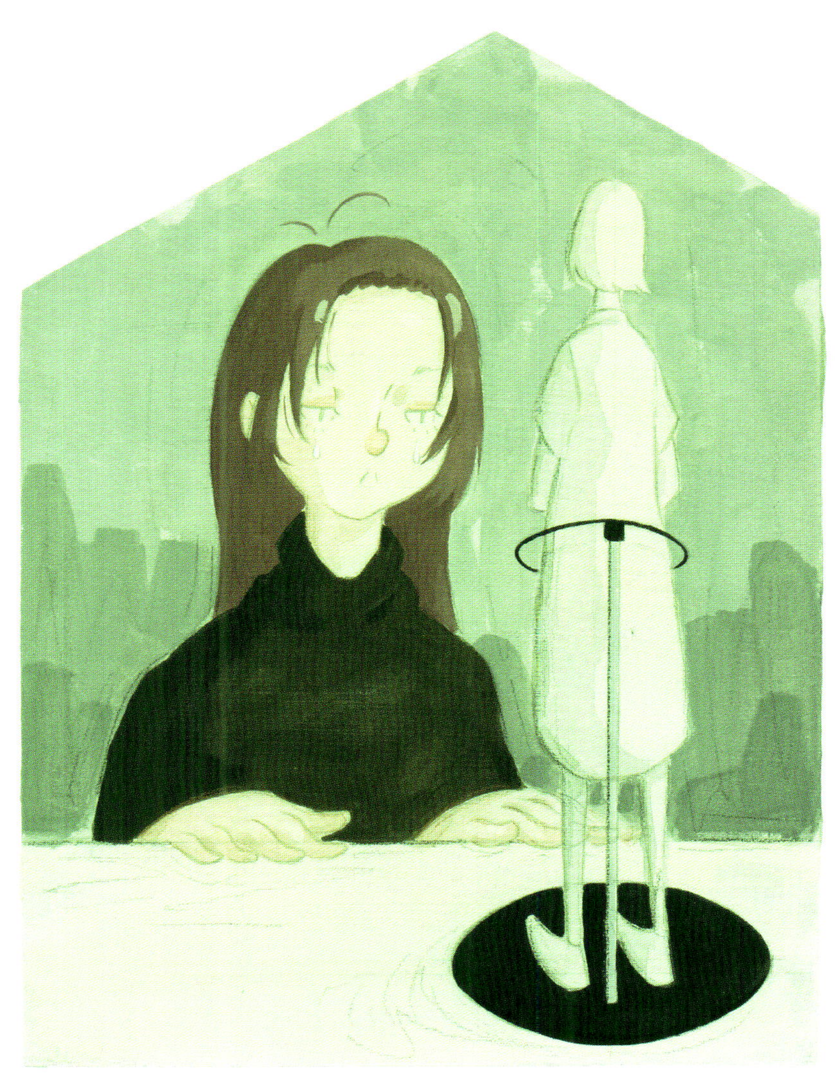

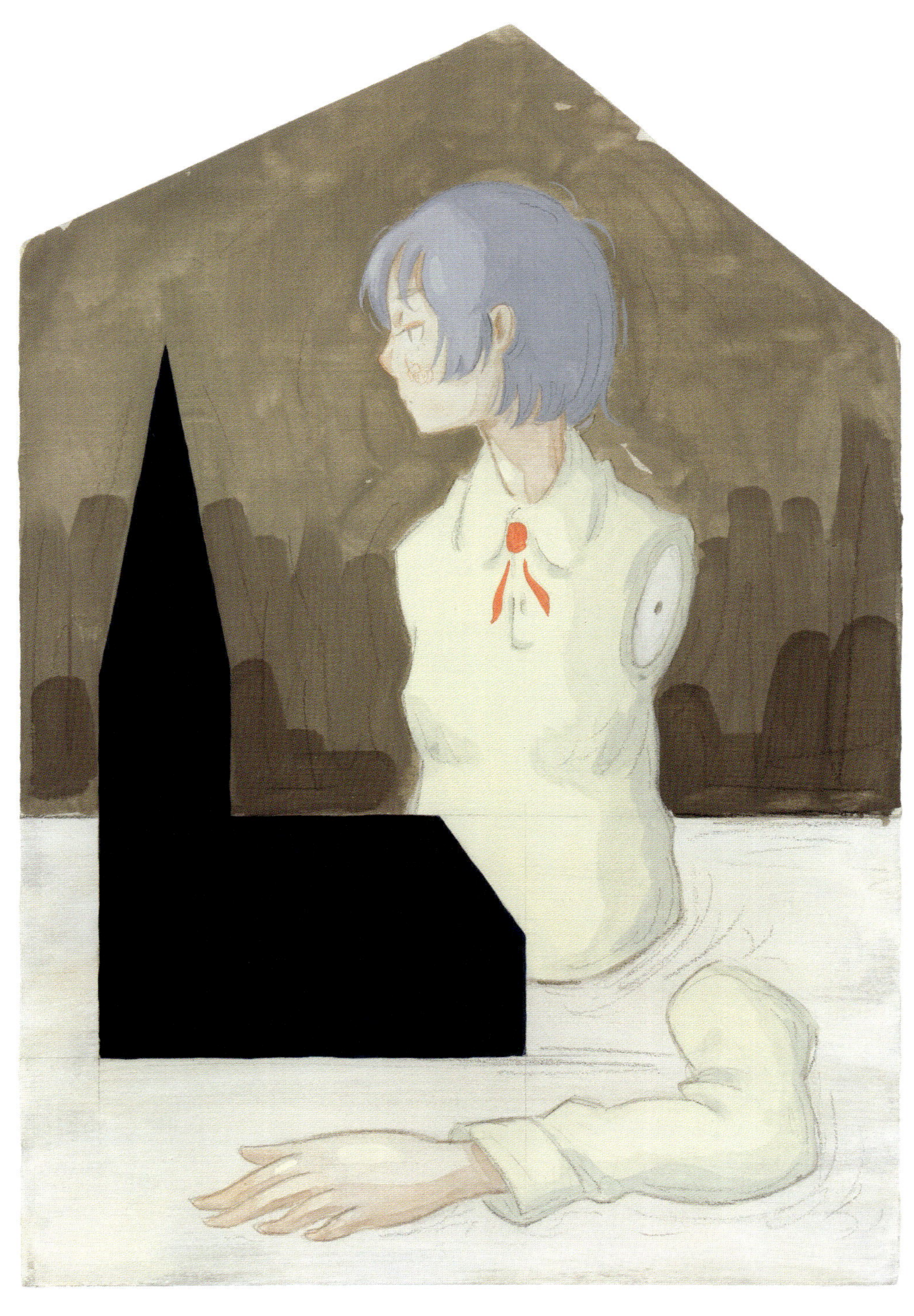

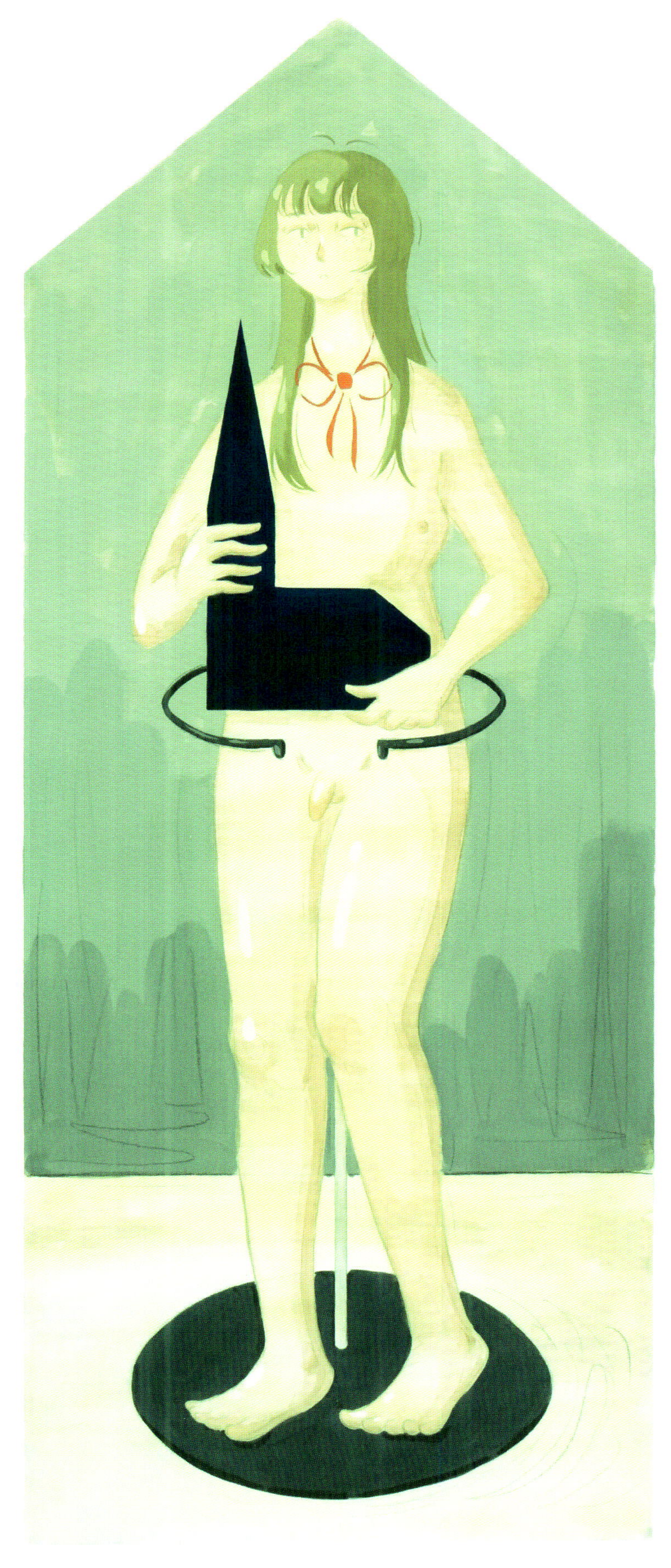

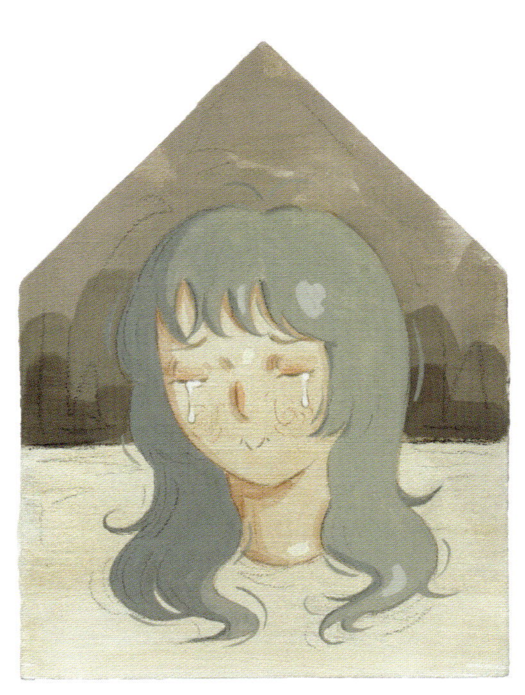

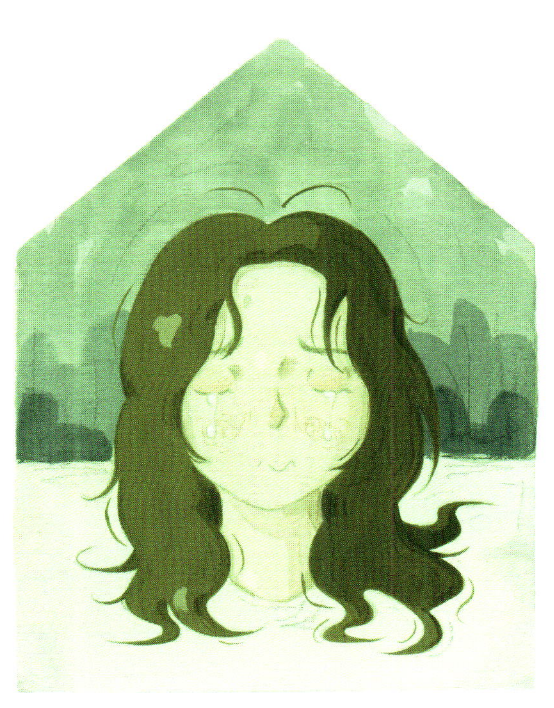

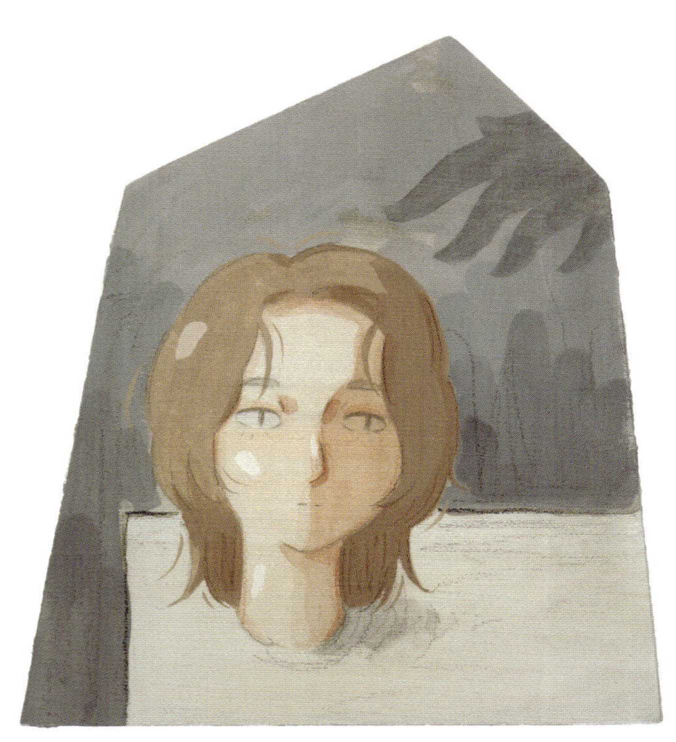

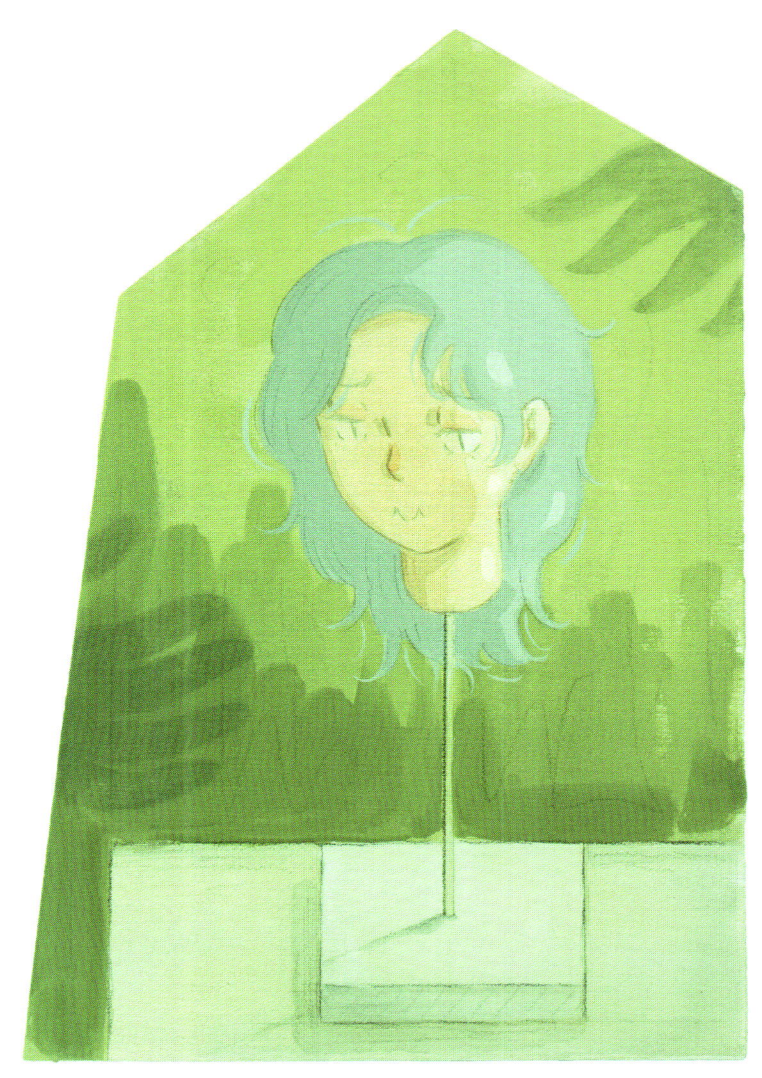

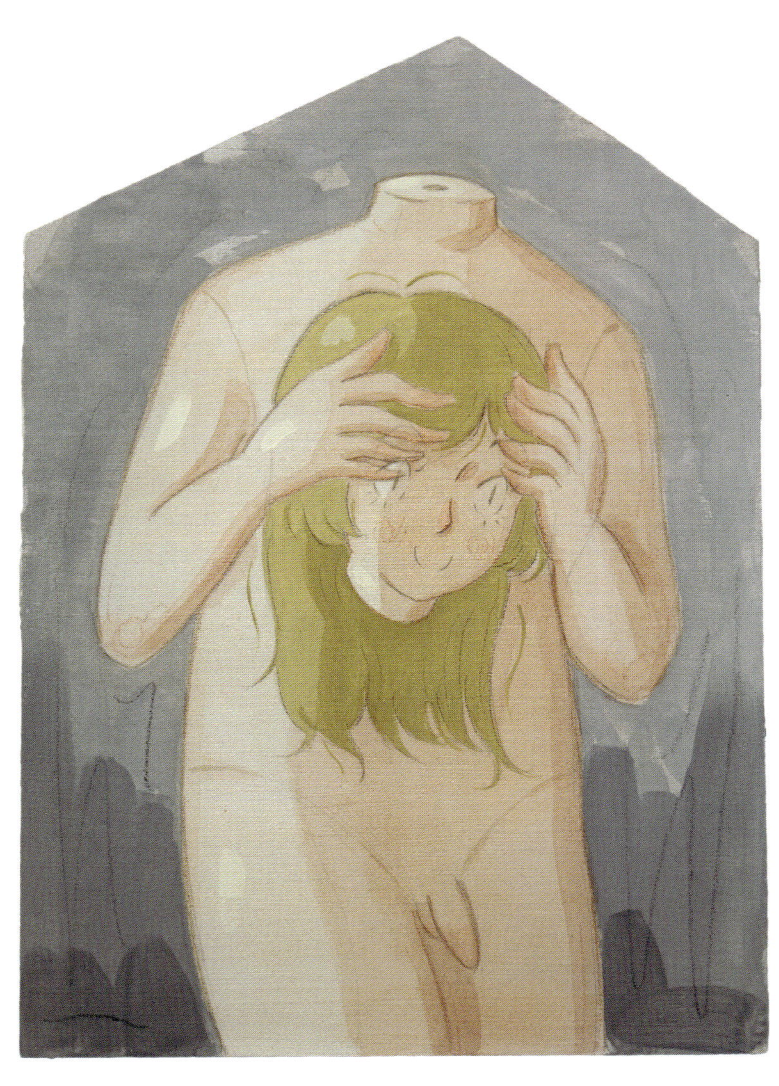

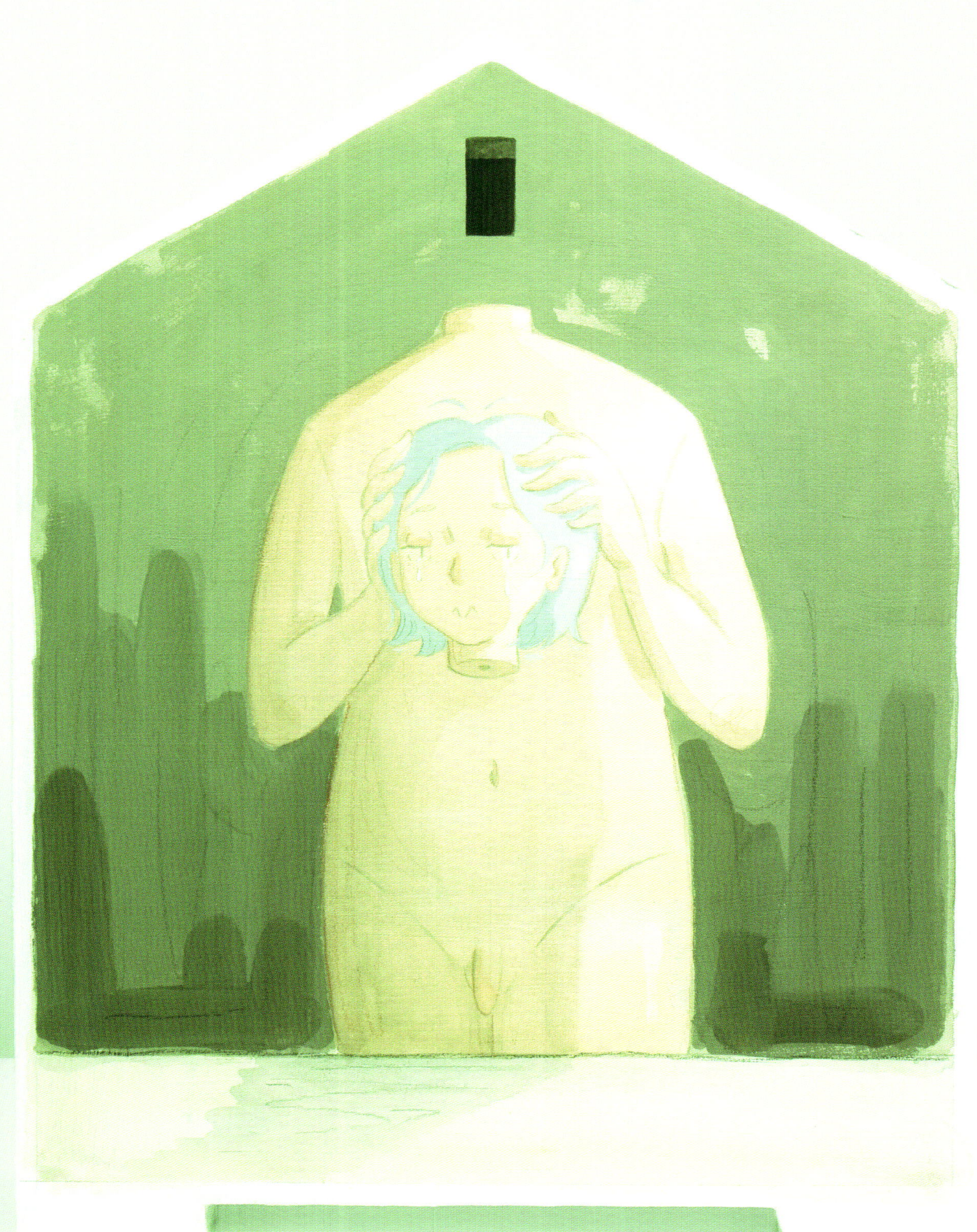

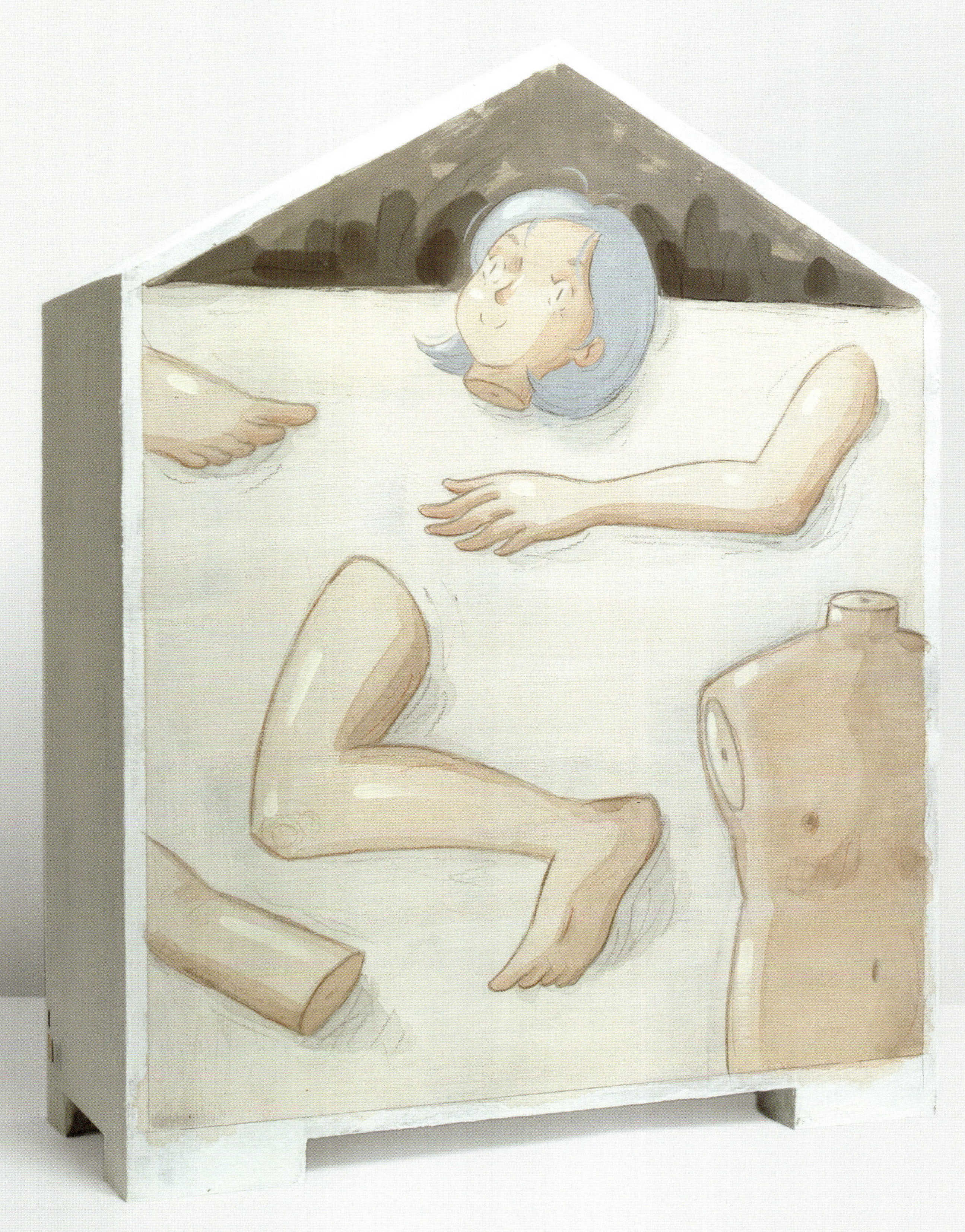

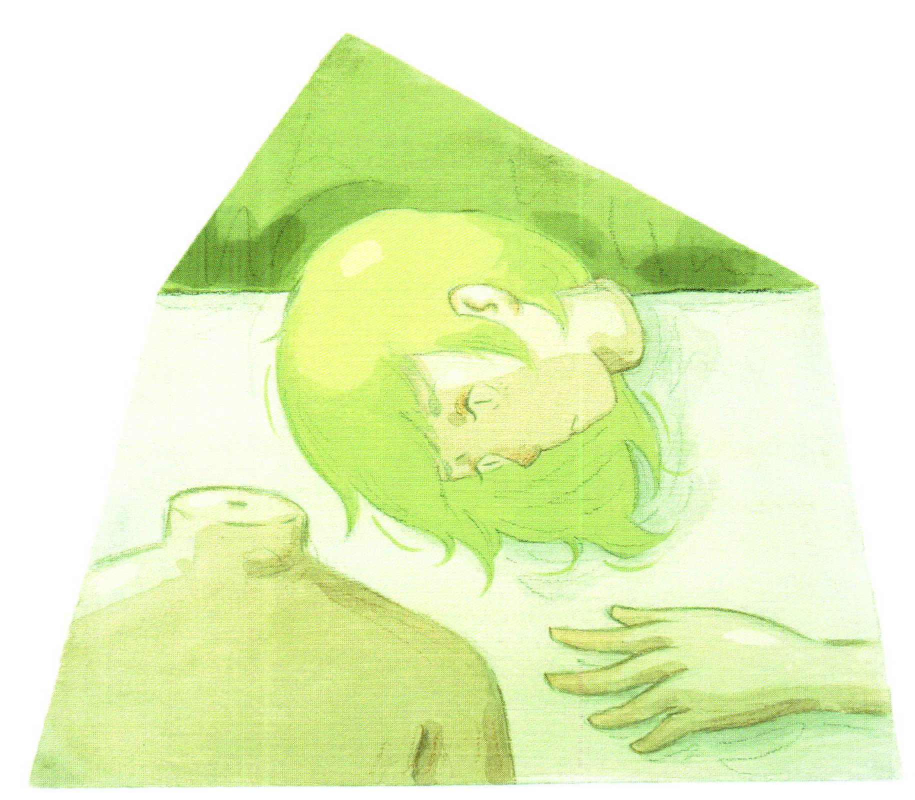

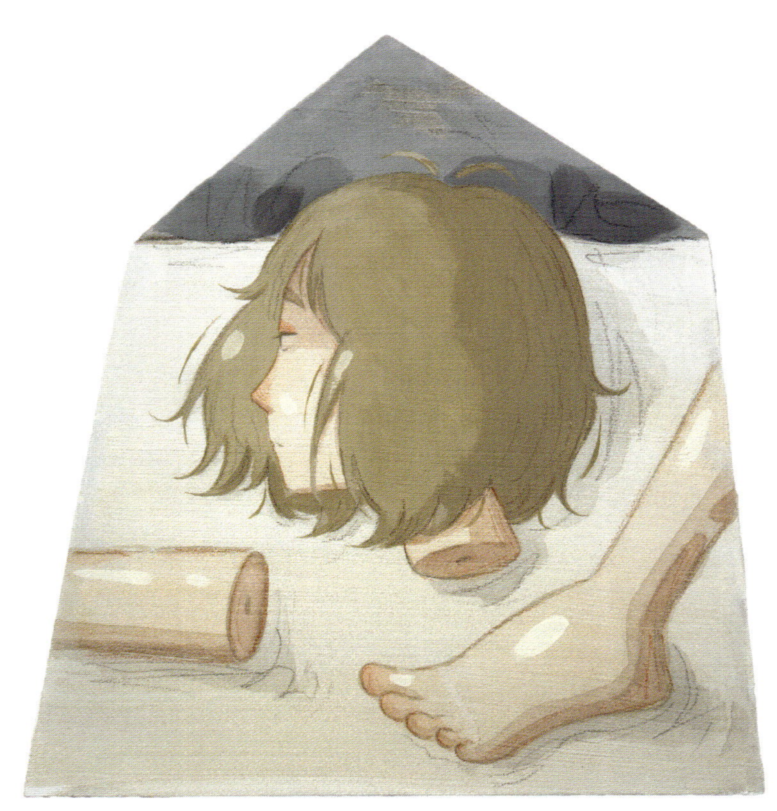

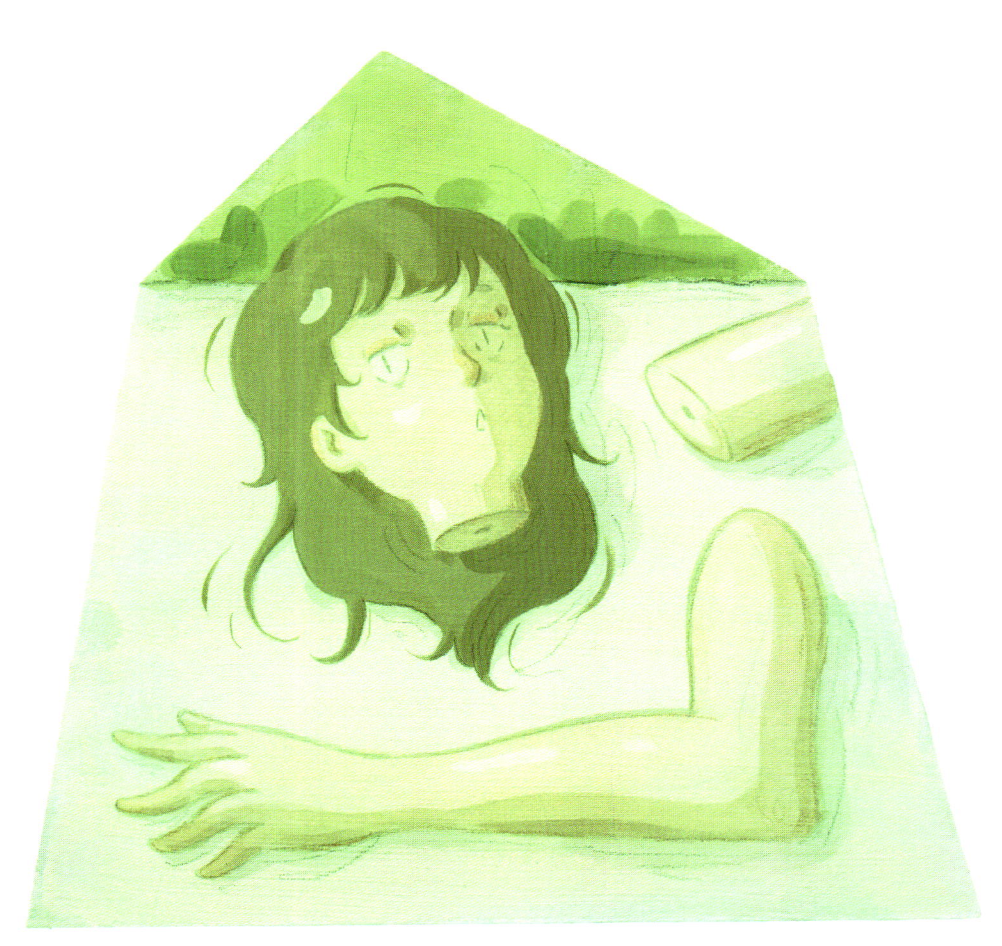

Afterword

I left Brugge, the historic medieval city where I was born, for the American suburbs in my early adolescence. The departure, in parallel with my puberty, felt like a rupture of my sense of belonging. I felt at home neither in my body nor in the alienating suburbs of Virginia. Years later, I returned to Belgium, just as I had started hormone replacement therapy in New York. My body was in flux, effectively entering a second puberty of sorts. These drastic physical and hormonal changes in my body seemed to go hand in hand with equally dramatic shifts in context. In this sense, I can't help but understand my body's history in relation to spatial, architectural displacement.

Brugge's art history, and by extension that of the early Renaissance period, has always lingered in my work. The compositions of the Flemish Primitives, and the many steeples adorning the Brugge skyline were ingrained in my early memories. However, coming back, I felt the weight of an insurmountable distance: between myself and the city, myself and those paintings, myself and an image of femininity I hadn't yet fully located in my body. While Brugge had remained as static as it ever had been in my absence, it no longer seemed to be able to hold space for me. The paintings in this book, in some ways, are a documentation of this distance, an attempt to give shape to my sense of gender and my feeling of perpetual placelessness.

I underwent several gender-affirming surgeries during the making of these works. To me, these surgeries served not only to approximate a sense of beauty but also to claim a corporeal sense of home. In a way, I had simply chosen to align my body with my work. However, in hindsight, it's also obvious that through these surgeries I was beginning to treat the body in my work as an architecture of sorts, something structural, occupiable, and alterable. I titled this book "The Dollhouse" thinking of this parallel between the figure and architecture. The title is also in dedication to all trans women (the "dolls"), to the character Rei Ayanami, and to Greer Lankton's doll club.

— Mae Dessauvage

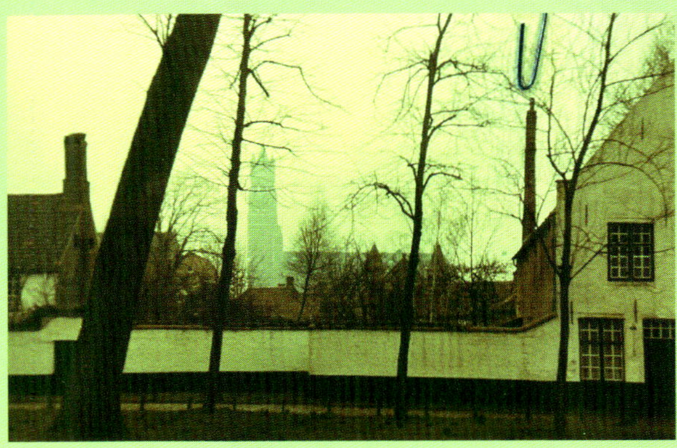

7　**Our Dear Lady**
2023
gouache, acrylic,
graphite and colored
pencil on panel
135 x 58cm

8-10　**Untitled I-XII**
2023
Gouache, acrylic,
graphite and colored
pencil on paper
21 x 15cm

11-12　**Revelation**
2023
Gouache, acrylic,
graphite and colored
pencil on panel
58 x 30 x 30cm

13　**Figure with Skull**
2024
Gouache, acrylic,
graphite and colored
pencil on panel
27 x 22cm

14　**Embrace**
2024
Gouache, acrylic,
graphite and colored
pencil on panel
28.5 x 24cm

15　**Two Figures with Orb**
2024
Gouache, acrylic,
graphite and colored
pencil on panel
27.5 x 23cm

16　**Figure with Orb**
2024
Gouache, acrylic,
graphite and colored
pencil on panel
27.5 x 20cm

17　**Figure with Church**
2024
Gouache, acrylic,
graphite and colored
pencil on panel
28.5 x 23cm

18　**Two Figures with Lily**
2024
Gouache, acrylic,
graphite and colored
pencil on panel
39 x 30.5cm

19　**Haunted Figure I**
2024
Gouache, acrylic,
graphite and colored
pencil on panel
26.5 x 17.5cm

20　**Haunted Figure II**
2024
Gouache, acrylic,
graphite and colored
pencil on panel
28 x 17.5cm

21　**Haunted Figure III**
2024
Gouache, acrylic,
graphite and colored
pencil on panel
27 x 19cm

22　**Haunted Figure IV**
2024
Gouache, acrylic,
graphite and colored
pencil on panel
23.5 x 16cm

23-24　**Intimacy**
2024
Gouache, acrylic,
graphite and colored
pencil on panel
28 x 16 x 6cm

25　**Intimidation**
2025
Gouache, acrylic,
graphite and colored
pencil on panel
44 x 30cm

26　**Composure**
2025
Gouache, acrylic,
graphite and colored
pencil on panel
71.5 x 40cm

27　**Concession**
2025
Gouache, acrylic,
graphite and colored
pencil on panel
56 x 38cm

28-30　**Shadow Play**
2024
Gouache, acrylic,
graphite and colored
pencil on panel
55.5 x 28 x 28cm

31　**Confrontation**
2024
Gouache, acrylic,
graphite and colored
pencil on panel
75.5 x 36.5cm

32　**Doll I**
2024
Gouache, acrylic,
graphite and colored
pencil on panel
30.5 x 20cm

33　**Doll II**
2025
Gouache, acrylic,
graphite and colored
pencil on panel
32.5 x 22cm

34 **Doll III**
2025
Gouache, acrylic,
graphite and colored
pencil on panel
32 x 21cm

35 **Humiliation**
2025
Gouache, acrylic,
graphite and colored
pencil on panel
83 x 35.5cm

36 **Figure with Doll I**
2025
Gouache, acrylic,
graphite and colored
pencil on panel
34 x 22cm

37 **Figure with Doll II**
2025
Gouache, acrylic,
graphite and colored
pencil on panel
39.5 x 23cm

38 **Figure with Doll III**
2025
Gouache, acrylic,
graphite and colored
pencil on panel
57.5 x 30cm

39 **Figure with Doll IV**
2025
Gouache, acrylic,
graphite and colored
pencil on panel
29.5 x 22cm

40 **Doll Parts with Church**
2025
Gouache, acrylic,
graphite and colored
pencil on panel
42.5 x 28.5cm

41 **Doll with Church**
2025
Gouache, acrylic,
graphite and colored
pencil on panel
162.5 x 65cm

42 **Doll Head I**
2025
Gouache, acrylic,
graphite and colored
pencil on panel
19 x 14cm

43 **Doll Head II**
2025
Gouache, acrylic,
graphite and colored
pencil on panel
18.5 x 14cm

44 **Haunted Doll Head I**
2025
Gouache, acrylic,
graphite and colored
pencil on panel
19.5 x 17.5cm

45 **Haunted Doll Head II**
2025
Gouache, acrylic,
graphite and colored
pencil on panel
29.5 x 20cm

46 **Doll with Head**
2025
Gouache, acrylic,
graphite and colored
pencil on panel
29 x 20cm

47-48 **Reconfiguration**
2025
Gouache, acrylic,
graphite and colored
pencil on panel
46 x 36 x 14cm

49 **Doll Parts I**
2025
Gouache, acrylic,
graphite and colored
pencil on panel
21.5 x 24cm

50 **Doll Parts II**
2025
Gouache, acrylic,
graphite and colored
pencil on panel
22 x 20.5cm

51 **Doll Parts III**
2025
Gouache, acrylic,
graphite and colored
pencil on panel
25 x 26cm

Mae Dessauvage
The Dollhouse

Published by Blurring Books
BlurringBooks.com / @BlurringBooksNYC

Courtesy TATJANA PIETERS

Artist Portrait by Finn Constantine
Revelation I-IV photos by Dirk Pauwels

Cover: Figure with Doll I, 2024, Mae Dessauvage

Special thanks to DB Burkeman, Sean Johnson, Tatjana
Pieters, Philippe van Cauteren, Isabel Chun and all
collectors

Printed in the U.K. in Carbon Neutral® facility

ISBN: 978-1-963814-29-3

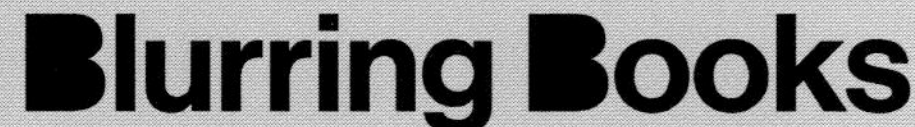

Blurring Books